THE REAL READERS' QUARTERLY

Slightly Foxed

'The Pram in the Hall'

NO.69   SPRING 2021

Editors Gail Pirkis & Hazel Wood
Marketing and publicity Stephanie Allen & Jennie Harrison Bunning
Bookshops Anna Kirk
Subscriptions Hattie Summers & Jess Dalby

Cover illustration: Niki Bowers, '"Spring Green" Tulips', linocut
Niki Bowers trained and worked for many years as a graphic designer,
later turning to printmaking. Using traditional methods, linocut prints are
made from multiple blocks, hand-cut and printed in limited editions.
These original prints reflect the landscape and wildlife of her native rural
Norfolk. Plant forms both wild and cultivated find their way into most
prints. To see more, please visit www.nikibowers.co.uk.
Cover fox: John Buckland-Wright

Design by Octavius Murray

Layout by Andrew Evans

Colophon and tailpiece by David Eccles

Published by Slightly Foxed Limited
53 Hoxton Square
London N1 6PB

tel 020 7033 0258
email office@foxedquarterly.com
www.foxedquarterly.com

Slightly Foxed is published quarterly in early March, June, September and December

Annual subscription rates (4 issues)
UK and Ireland £48; Overseas £56

Single copies of this issue can be bought for £12.50 (UK) or £14.50 (Overseas)

All back issues in printed form are also available

ISBN 978-1-910898-54-3
ISSN 1742-5794

Printed and bound by Smith Settle, Yeadon, West Yorkshire

Contents

Contents

The Slightly Foxed Podcast

A new episode of our podcast is available on the 15th of every month. To listen, visit www.foxedquarterly.com/pod or search for Slightly Foxed on Audioboom, iTunes or your podcast app.

Subscriber Benefits

Slightly Foxed can obtain any books reviewed in this issue, whether new or second-hand. To enquire about a book, to access the digital edition of *Slightly Foxed* or to view a list of membership benefits, visit www.foxedquarterly.com/members or contact the office: 020 7033 0258/office@foxedquarterly.com.

From the Editors

How cheering it is to see that there are signs of spring now both in the air and in the step of the people walking along Old Street and in the little streets around Hoxton Square. It feels as if Londoners are tentatively starting to pick up the threads of their lives again. As we've reported before, life in the Slightly Foxed office has not in fact been so very different during this last extraordinary year, except perhaps that we've been busier than usual – support from you for which we'll be forever grateful. Anna, Hattie and Jess have been brilliant at keeping the show on the road, whatever the restrictions, and now Jennie is back with us from maternity leave – another reason to be cheerful.

We're full of publishing plans for 2021, and for another series of podcasts. These have struck a note with so many of you during a year in which most of us yearned for companionable conversation and the feeling of normality and continuity that talk about books and writers can bring. In the autumn the *Spectator*'s reviewer described our podcast as 'muskily lovely . . . the sort of thing you can imagine listening to with a dog at your feet and a whisky at your side', praising the cosy and calming atmosphere and the fact that we allow our guests to have their say before plying them with questions. This is probably because we're so genuinely fascinated by them and what they're saying, on subjects which have ranged from garden writing to the workings of a small publisher.

For those of you who enjoyed our winter Slightly Foxed Edition *Cider with Rosie*, perhaps rediscovering this magical book after many years, our new spring SFE continues Laurie Lee's autobiographical trilogy. In *As I Walked Out One Midsummer Morning* he describes how at the age of 19 he said goodbye to his Cotswold childhood and set out on foot to see the world with only his violin for company (see p.12). So began a year of wandering that took him to London and then on foot through Spain, from Vigo in the north down to the Mediterranean. It's a dark and brooding picture of a country still trapped in the Middle Ages but hovering on the brink of revolution. For Lee his journey wasn't simply a coming of age but an experience that marked him for ever and drew him back to Spain again to fight on the Republican side in the Civil War.

New out in our Cubs series is *Dawn Wind*, the next of Rosemary Sutcliff's wonderful novels recreating early Britain from the last years of the Roman occupation into the mysterious period known as the Dark Ages (see p.59). Its young hero Owain, who has both British and Roman blood in his veins, is the sole human survivor of a terrible battle with the Saxons, and his struggles are another, though very different, coming-of-age story. Sutcliff has the most astonishing gift for breathing life into her characters, both human and animal, and for evoking an atmosphere that lingers in the mind – entering a little early Christian church, Owain is met by 'a whisper of incense, mingled with the smell of age and shadows'. We have both read *Dawn Wind* and the other books in the series several times in the process of reissuing them, and they never pall.

And finally, our congratulations to Frances Keeton of Dundee, the winner of our twelfth annual crossword competition, who receives a free annual subscription. For those of you still foxed by some of the clues, the answers are on p.95.

GAIL PIRKIS & HAZEL WOOD

John Watson

The Pram in the Hall

LAURA FREEMAN

'Neither a borrower nor a lender be,' my grandfather used to say gravely. His caution wasn't about money. It was about books. Do not lend a book you will want back and do not borrow one you will be sorry to return. Sound advice. Not that I've kept to it. Some books I am willing to relinquish. That makes space on my heaving shelves. The loss of others I mourn.

I lent my copy of Barbara Hepworth's *A Pictorial Autobiography* to an illustrator friend who, for reasons of distance and diaries, I rarely see. We had been talking about children and creativity and whether one must necessarily restrict the other: the easel, the laptop, the pram in the hall. I said she must read Hepworth and posted her my copy. It arrived. She thanked me. After that: nothing. Nothing for months and months and a year, and for months after that. I nursed a perverse and very British grievance. I couldn't possibly ask for it back, because that would be rude. Instead, I did the proper and polite thing of raining resentment, curses and hellfire on her head every time my eye caught the gap in the bookcase.

As the second anniversary of the lending approached, I shrugged, shuffled the shelf and wrote the book off as a loss. Then, in the way of watched pots never boiling, the book came back with a hand-painted card and a note. She was sorry she'd kept it, but she'd wanted to read it again and again. 'Hepworth is *so right*,' she wrote. I cherish my copy all the more now, like a stone that has been skimmed on the

Barbara Hepworth, *A Pictorial Autobiography* (1970)
Tate Publishing · Pb · 136pp · £14.99 · ISBN 9781854371492

ocean and which, in defiance of time and tide, has at last come skimming back.

Barbara Hepworth was a sculptor, not a writer. Her tools weren't pen and paper, but chisel and stone. *A Pictorial Autobiography* is really a scrapbook. There are family photos, school certificates, college diplomas, reproductions of works, gallery pamphlets, press cuttings and assorted archive riflings. We see the infant Barbara in a white smock become Barbara the art student in long beads and split sleeves, become Mrs John Skeaping, sculptor wife to a sculptor husband, become Miss Hepworth, the exhibiting artist, become Mrs Ben Nicholson, mother to triplets, and, at the end of her life, Dame Barbara in workman's overalls and silk headscarf. There are enchanting contrasts: standing stones and wobbling toddlers, the Venice Biennale and bare, knobbly knees on the beach.

The book is like one of Hepworth's stringed sculptures with threads of text tying the photographs together. (A cartoon clipped from a magazine shows Hepworth seated at a sculpture that looks like an old Singer sewing-machine, pulling a needle through the tops and the sides.) She starts with her childhood in the West Riding, driving through and over the hills in her father's car, seeing for the first time 'the hollow, the thrust and the contour' of landscape. We meet her again at Wakefield Girls' High School with its 'gorgeous smell' of paint. 'My headmistress knew I detested sports and games,' Hepworth writes. 'I loved dancing, music, drawing and painting. And wonderfully, when all had departed to the playing fields I found myself miraculously alone with easel, paints and paper in the school.' We follow her to Leeds School of Art, the Royal College of Art in London, on a scholarship to Rome, Florence and Siena, to Belsize Park, Hampstead, Paris, Provence and to St Ives where her endless hammering draws endless complaints from the neighbours.

The book is like her sculpture in another way, too: it is full of holes. Having married John Skeaping in the Palazzo Vecchio in Florence on p.13 and given birth to their son Paul on p.17 – 'this was

8

An artist and her tools:
Barbara Hepworth at the
Trewyn Studio, St Ives

a wonderfully happy time' – two lines later she writes: 'Quite suddenly we were out of orbit. I had an obsession for my work and my
child and my home. John wanted to go free, and he bought a horse
which used to breathe through my kitchen window!' And that is that.
John is gone. It is the same with her marriage to Ben Nicholson.
They meet in 1931, they have the triplets Simon, Rachel and Sarah
in 1934, they marry in 1938, there is the war, they move to St Ives,
and then, 'In 1951, after twenty years of family life, everything was to
fall apart.' No more. Visitors to Trewyn Studio, now the Barbara
Hepworth Museum and Sculpture Garden in St Ives, are almost
obliged to take a picture peering through the space in one of
Hepworth's bronzes, as if it were a seaside photo-board with circles
cut out for the faces of pirate and mermaid. Readers of Hepworth's
Pictorial Autobiography find themselves peering through holes in the
story, discovering voids where there ought to be form.

But this is Hepworth's story and she tells it in her own way. She began by gathering photographs but found they made the book too personal. She asked her son-in-law Alan Bowness, art historian and husband to Sarah, if he would help. It was Bowness who rooted out the reviews, the catalogues, the photographs of casts and plasters, which made the book, first published in 1970, 'more work than life, which was what she wanted'.

Never mind the holes and withholdings. The fascination of the book, what drew me to it when I first leafed through the pages in the gift shop of Tate Britain's exhibition 'Barbara Hepworth: Sculpture for a Modern World', is sharing in what Hepworth does reveal: how to be an artist, a wife, a mother, a grandmother. How to strike a balance between family life and the life of the mind. How to bear it when the scales can't and won't be made to balance. She admits that when the one baby she had thought she was carrying turned out to be three ('Shut up, Ben, this is no time for jokes,' said their friends when Nicholson rang with the news), she 'knew fear' for the first time in her life. How was she to support a family of four children – 5-year-old Paul and three newborns – on her carvings and on Ben's white reliefs? How would she make time to make anything at all? What was she without her work?

Anyone who has ever counted down to a holiday with the thought: 'Oh, good, now I can really get some painting/writing/thinking done!' will recognize the rapture with which Hepworth writes of 'working holidays'. This habit was established by childhood summers at Robin Hood's Bay. She had a room in the attic and 'here I laid out my paints and general paraphernalia and crept out at dawn to collect stones, seaweeds and paint, and draw by myself before somebody organized me!' These working weeks by the sea, she writes,

> made a firm foundation for my working life – and it formed my ideas that a woman artist is not deprived by cooking and having children, nor by nursing children with measles (even in triplicate)

– one is in fact nourished by this rich life, provided one always does some work each day; even a single half hour, so that the images grow in one's mind.

I detest a day of no work, no music, no poetry.

It is these words that struck a chord. They were the words I wanted my friend to read. I am 32. Over and over, I have the same debate: books or babies or both? When I first went freelance five years ago, a friend who had had three children in her early twenties said how wonderful it was that I would never need to bother about an au pair or a nanny: 'You can just bounce the baby on your knee as you write.' I said yes, so as not to argue, but thought to myself: there speaks a woman who has never tried to write a steady thousand words a day. Another friend, also a mother of three children, aged 6, 4 and 20 months, had different advice. I had said I was in awe of how many new novels she managed to read. There was an hour each weekday when the two older children were at school and the youngest child was having her nap. 'I decided I could use that time to tidy up,' she said, amid the chaos of the kitchen, 'or I could use it to read my book.'

As wife, mother and sculptor, Hepworth got it right and she got it wrong, but she got some work done every day. I have lost count of the number of books and articles I have read telling me to lean in and get on and rise up and be the boss and smash the ceiling and beat the boys. None have stayed with me as Hepworth has, none have done so much to inspire and spur and reassure. 'Even a single half hour.' The words are carved on my heart.

LAURA FREEMAN is writing a biography of Jim Ede and the Kettle's Yard artists, one of whom is Barbara Hepworth.

Before the Slaughter

JUSTIN MAROZZI

How much we miss movement in our suddenly still, stay-at-home pandemic era. Gone the footloose and fancy-free travel of our rose-tinted imaginations, replaced by domestic gloom, pessimistic prospects and shrinking horizons. There seems something pleasingly necessary, then, about revisiting one of the great literary road trips, which celebrates movement for the sake of it and revels in youthful, devil-may-care vagabondism in a Europe basking in its last years of peace.

Not for Laurie Lee a narrowing world of masks, Covid tests and self-isolation. In 1935, staring across the rooftops of London, the 20-year-old made a life-changing discovery: 'I could go anywhere I liked in the world. There was nothing to stop me, I would be penniless, free and could just pack up and walk away.' Europe was wide open, 'a place of casual frontiers, no questions and almost no travellers'. Bliss, in other words.

The road trip, in fact, had begun the previous year. Shaking off the bucolic Gloucestershire childhood in Slad which, decades later, he conjured up in *Cider with Rosie*, the teenager resolved to walk to London but, never having set eyes on the sea, he did so via the south coast. Armed only with a violin and a walking stick, he quickly realized that busking could pay the bills. 'Those first days in Southampton were a kind of obsession; I was out in the streets from morning till night, moving from pitch to pitch in a gold-dust fever, playing till the tips of my fingers burned.' In just over an hour one day, he earned 38 shillings, 'more than a farm-labourer earned in a week'. It stood him in good stead for the long journey ahead.

This is all knockabout, high-spirited adolescence, but the older

Lee was writing decades after his escapades as a pedestrian, just as his contemporary Patrick Leigh Fermor recalled his own walk from the Hook of Holland to Constantinople through adult eyes more than forty years afterwards in *A Time of Gifts* and *Between the Woods and the Water*. Here, in *As I Walked Out One Midsummer Morning*, first published in 1969, Lee is sufficiently self-aware to understand that there was much more to life on the road than youthful japes and innocent fun. While the young man 'pretended I was T. E. Lawrence, engaged in some self-punishing odyssey', the later Lee wrote with empathy about those trudging the English roads in the 1930s not out of some frivolous dream of adventure but from the imperative of survival. This was the 'host of unemployed . . . a broken army walking away from a war, cheeks sunken, eyes dead with fatigue'.

Here as elsewhere Lee makes a little language go a long way. The poet's prose may be rich and well-formed but rarely, if ever, does it tip into the ornate baroque of Leigh Fermor. A sentence, or even a clause, can lay claim to an entire world. In London where, saving up for his adventure, he spends a year pushing barrows of wet cement alongside his fellow builder's labourers, he writes affectionately of a motley collection of safe-breakers, cat-men, dopers, a forger, a bigamist and a rapist. The description teeters on the romantic before reality bites. Each man, he writes, is 'shrivelled by years of attrition, by the staleness of poverty, doubt and suspicion, and by the diminishing returns of jail'.

For anyone who has read *Cider with Rosie*, Lee's descriptive powers require little introduction. In this second volume in the trilogy they are on display within the first few pages. The sea is 'a great sweep of curved nothing rolling out to the invisible horizon . . . revealing more distance than I'd ever seen before. It was green, and heaved gently like the skin of a frog, and carried drowsy little ships like flies.'

The pen portraits ring with humour and resonate with accumulated detail. Every evening his Cockney landlady Mrs Flynn emerges 'in laminated gold, with silkily reconditioned hair, to engage the

Leonard Rosoman

world in a monologue of bubbling non-sequiturs, full of giggles, regrets and yearnings', describing the Richmond deer 'wearing their beautiful antelopes' and offering her views on 'the Russian revulsion'.

So with the world on his doorstep, where did Lee go? He chose Spain, he tells us, for no other reason than that he knew how to say, 'Will you please give me a glass of water?' in Spanish. Why not? It is as good a reason as any. Landing on the Atlantic coast at Vigo, he heads inland for his first night under the stars, observing from the hills a dark, glittering coastline that looks 'like sweepings of broken glass'. On his way to Zamora he sleeps in a ruined castle next to the skeleton of a sheep picked clean 'like a wicker basket'. The days soon blur into 'a continuous movement of sun and shadow, hunger and thirst, fatigue and sleep', leavened by a steady flow of Spanish hospitality.

Look at a map of Lee's wanderings across Spain and you get a striking sense of the spirit in which he made them. This is no linear journey from A to B. It is instead the most languid, alphabetical curve unfurling across the Iberian Peninsula, from the Atlantic coast into the Galician heartland, on to Valladolid, through the sun-baked delirium and 'electric haze of heat' of the Castilian plain, then south over the Guadarramas, from Segovia to Seville via Madrid and Toledo, across the Sierra Morena into Andalusia and then south again to Cádiz before squiggling again, this time east along the Mediterranean coast, to Tarifa, Málaga and Almuñécar. It took him a year.

Crossing the interminable Castilian plain, he watches harvest-workers strung across the fields like butterflies. 'Submerged in the wheat, sickles flickered like fish, with rhythmic flashes of blue and silver.' He confesses to experiencing 'that faint sour panic' when arriving in an unknown city without having found a bed for the night. Yet time and again the quick-witted traveller pulls out his violin, earns himself a few pesetas, a bowl of seafood here, a glass of brandy there, and secures his roost. Wine is a constant companion on the road, shared with peasants and fishermen, beggars and ne'er-do-wells. Like the most interesting travellers Lee opens himself to all the experiences of the road, to all the people and places he encounters, from priests to prostitutes, from dismal Valladolid to his final destination of Almuñécar (disguised as 'Castillo' to protect the villagers), where in 1936 he inhales the first heady whiff of the Spanish Civil War.

Footsore and virtually penniless, he eyes the rich from a distance while breaking bread with the poor. Though he knows nothing of Spain on arrival, by the time he leaves he has managed to gulp down the soul of the country through this street-level immersion. Again and again the itinerant fiddler offers closely observed portraits of the suffering indigent, especially the beggars of the cities through which he passes, 'creatures of every imaginable curse and deformity' and 'mute concentrations of martyrdom'. If *Cider with Rosie* is too idealized for some readers, then this later book does not shrink from confronting the ugliness of poverty, from the drunken landlord trying to rape his daughter to downtrodden, serf-like villagers simmering in southern revolution.

Lee was a crowd-pleaser from a young age, a talent that never left him as he held court into his dotage before admirers who had made the pilgrimage to The Woolpack Inn in Slad to see him. Half a century later his prose still gives great pleasure – and for the most part it is timeless. Reading him can often feel like a guilty indulgence. Perhaps the only off-key moments, sharpened by our knowledge of Lee's famously wandering eye and his highly controlling behaviour towards the various women in his life, especially his daughter Jessy, come in his physical descriptions of girls and women: a would-be girlfriend in London is 'a smooth leggy figure, lithe as an Indian pony', another is 'heart-stoppingly voluptuous in her tight Californian pants', while in Toledo he dreams drunkenly of 'silken thighs'.

As I Walked Out One Midsummer Morning marks the stylistic as well as the chronological midpoint between the light-filled lushness of *Cider with Rosie* and the darker, honed-to-the-bone economy of *A Moment of War*. Here, as Lee bids farewell to the retreating coastline of Spain, he can still smell 'its runnels of dust, the dead ash of its fields, whiffs of sour wine, rotting offal and incense . . .' He retreads 'the great gold plains, the arid mystical distances, where the sun rose up like a butcher each morning and left curtains of blood each night'. With the final promise of 'a winter of war', he warns us there will be more blood to come.

JUSTIN MAROZZI loves a long walk.

Laurie Lee's *As I Walked Out One Midsummer Morning* (240pp), illustrated by Leonard Rosoman, is now available in a limited and numbered cloth-bound edition of 2,000 copies (subscribers: UK & Eire £17, Overseas £19; non-subscribers: UK & Eire £18.50, Overseas £20.50). All prices include post and packing. Copies may be ordered by post (53 Hoxton Square, London N1 6PB), by phone (020 7033 0258) or via our website www.foxedquarterly.com.

Growing Pains

MARTIN SORRELL

An annual pre-Christmas treat for me is discovering which books have impressed the great and the good of the literary world over the previous twelve months. The lists in the heavyweight papers invariably give me two or three ideas for spending the book tokens I know are coming my way. One year Ian McEwan praised John Williams's *Stoner*, which I found so strong that I didn't hesitate a few years later to follow up another of McEwan's recommendations, the more so as he wasn't alone in picking it. At least two other contributors had been struck by *Reunion*, a novella of under a hundred pages written by Fred Uhlman, a German-Jewish painter and writer. When it was first published in 1971 *Reunion* went unnoticed; and though it was a little more successful when reissued a few years later, it wasn't until a further reissue in 2015 that it was recognized as the masterpiece it is.

My tokens came, and as soon as the shops opened again I bought a copy. It looked an ideal read for the awkward days between Christmas and the New Year, but by the tenth page I was wondering whether to go on. It seemed far too close to that celebrated and painful account of growing up and losing paradise, Alain-Fournier's *Le Grand Meaulnes*. I didn't want either to read the same story again or to stir poignant memories of my parents, still missed after so long. On our way to my mother's native Auvergne they'd taken me through the area where Alain-Fournier set his novel, the enigmatic Sologne.

But curiosity got the better of me. I fetched myself a glass of

---

Fred Uhlman, *Reunion* (1971)
Harvill · Pb · 96pp · £7.99 · ISBN 9781860463655

mulled wine, settled back, opened *Reunion* at the next chapter, and read on. I needn't have hesitated. The elegant prose was a delight. It was hard to believe that someone whose first language wasn't English could write it so well. Uhlman must have written in German, surely, and been translated. Apparently not. Over the years his English had become as stylish as that of two other non-native masters of the language who came to mind, Conrad and Nabokov. Hooked, I read straight through to the end, with its startling twist. (Warning: resist the urge to take a premature peek.)

It's February 1932. We're in Stuttgart, in a classroom of the school modelled on the one Uhlman himself attended. Among the class is the narrator, Hans Schwarz. He's just turned 16; he's clever, sensitive, a little bit bored, and he's Jewish. One day a boy from a completely different world arrives. Asked to give his name, he stands up and announces 'Graf von Hohenfels, Konradin'. His poise, his natural authority, in fact everything about him dazzles Hans. Partly, although it's never described in those terms, it looks like an adolescent crush; partly, it's the same snobbery that will later make Hans squirm when his father bows and fawns on meeting Konradin; but mostly, it's that Hans has sensed he's a kindred spirit, and he determines to make Konradin his friend.

Difficult, you'd think, given that Hans is a needy middle-class Jew and Konradin a proud Aryan from a thousand-year-old noble family so illustrious that even the President of the Republic bows to them. Nevertheless, Hans tries his best. In one memorable scene he shows off his gymnastic skills, like a medieval jouster out to win a princess. Eventually Konradin thaws. It turns out the two boys have much in common. They discuss poetry, philosophy; they compare book and coin collections, go to the opera, take trips together. It's a friendship so intense I wondered how it could last. Sooner or later, something would wreck it, surely. Girls?

In my teens I too formed an unlikely bond with a lad from school. He was thoroughly English and Home Counties, I a half-French country boy. He lived in a villa with a tennis-court, I in a terrace with a backyard. Our friendship was sealed the afternoon I found him cradling an injured baby rook. Slowly we nursed it back to health until one day it upped and left us. For a few more months our friendship grew, to the virtual exclusion of all others . . . until a girl called Gillian happened, and that was that.

Likewise, the friendship of Hans and Konradin falls apart, but not because of a girl. In the year since Konradin erupted into Hans's life, another story has been gathering pace: the rise of Hitler. With powerful understatement Uhlman weaves together the two stories, one intimate, the other nationwide. Big events are related from the confines of the two boys' lives. As the Nazis tighten their grip, Hans is increasingly persecuted at school; Konradin's virulently anti-Semitic mother won't have him in her house; and then Konradin reveals his own high hopes for Hitler and informs Hans that their friendship cannot continue. Actually, it's over anyway. Hans's parents, who've seen the future, have already decided to pack him off abroad to safety.

In many respects Uhlman's fate resembles that of Hans. In 1933 Uhlman fled to France, where he became a painter, although he'd originally trained for the law. Three years later he was in London, having married an English girl he'd met while living briefly in Spain. They had two children, and Uhlman continued to live happily in Britain with his family until his death almost fifty years later. As for Hans, he's dispatched to America, also in 1933. There he finishes his education, marries, becomes a father and makes a career as a lawyer. He's a citizen of the New World, living the American Dream. Old Europe is dead and buried.

Then one day, news arrives from his old school in Stuttgart and delivers the punch which ends *Reunion* – and which still knocks me sideways whenever I think about it.

Now that MARTIN SORRELL has at last found a copy of Uhlman's autobiography, he's keen to see what else of *Reunion* is there.

Lyndon B. Johnson, Dad and Me

ANDY MERRILLS

In the end, it was no surprise that I turned to books in the aftermath of my father's death; as much as anything else, a love of reading, and a confidence in the calming power of the written word, was one of the many things that he gave me. What was more unexpected was the identity of the book that offered the greatest solace.

My first ports of call were natural enough places to turn, and all of them did help. Dad was reading Jan Morris's tiny book on the vast Japanese battleship *Yamato* the day before he died, and so that was where I started. In later weeks I picked up James Agee's *A Death in the Family*, Max Porter's *Grief Is the Thing with Feathers* and William Wharton's extraordinary *Dad*, an author whom I love, but a book which I don't think I'll ever be able to pick up again without a great deal of pain.

Each of these rendered loss in terms that were helpful, and of course my reading of each was supercharged with a sort of hyper-sensitivity, and I think I left a little of my hurt in the pages of each of them. On the train to the funeral, I read Geoff Dyer's *Broadsword Calling Danny Boy*, about that iconic war film *Where Eagles Dare*, and laughed out loud much of the way there, which is not something I would have thought possible. But in some ways the book – or rather books – that did most to lift me out of the gloom came in the

---

The first four volumes of Robert Caro's biography of Lyndon B. Johnson – *The Path to Power* (1982), *Means of Ascent* (1990), *Master of the Senate* (2002) and *The Passage of Power* (2012) – are available in paperback from the Bodley Head.

most unexpected form: Robert Caro's four-volume (thus far) biography, *The Years of Lyndon Johnson*.

Caro's biography is undoubtedly one of the monuments of American political writing in the modern age. Consisting to date of *The Path to Power* (1982), *Means of Ascent* (1990), *Master of the Senate* (2002) and *The Passage of Power* (2012), the study traces the brutal political rise of Lyndon Baines Johnson from impoverished origins in the Texas hill country outside Austin to Washington DC, the House and the Senate, and on to his eventual position as running mate and Vice-President of John F. Kennedy. The staggered publication of the work testifies to the staggering scale of its ambition: each decade-long slab of research draws Johnson further along his path to the presidency, and the reader further into the peculiar world of the candidate himself. At the end of four books, and somewhere close to 3,500 pages, the story has only got as far as the 1964 election, the point at which Johnson truly made the presidency his own.

The next volume, we are promised, will take the reader through those febrile years until 1968 – the stamping of Johnsonian authority on Kennedy's crumbled Camelot, the passing of the most important Civil Rights legislation in American history, and of course the President's role in the deepening quagmire that was Vietnam.

Caro's work has been praised in all sorts of ways since its first publication, and each new volume amplifies this chorus. *The Path to Power* was celebrated as one of the most important political biographies of its time, *Master of the Senate* won Caro his second Pulitzer prize (his first was for the biography of the New York master-planner Robert Moses), and the cycle is routinely celebrated as an inspiration by people as diverse as Michael Howard and Barack Obama. As far as I know, though, *The Years of Lyndon Johnson* has yet to receive its due as a tonic for the bereaved. Perhaps that should change.

I should state from the outset that Lyndon Johnson had absolutely nothing in common with my father. In Caro's telling, Johnson was a deceitful, duplicitous bully who rose to power on the strength of fervent ambition. At every level of his ascent – from college politics to local administration, from the House to the Senate, and ultimately to the White House, Johnson secured his authority by combining a minute familiarity with administrative procedure, a terrifying competence and a genuine indifference to the feelings of those beneath him in the grand pecking order. He earned the fear and loyalty of countless underlings, many of whom he trampled over without much thought. He introduced new levels of outside campaign finances to American politics, and new levels of corruption too, making himself staggeringly rich in the process.

Lyndon B. Johnson, 1941

None of this was true of Dad. While he was proud of reaching a relatively high level in his university department, and could occasionally go into too much detail when talking about board games, it would be a stretch to call him ruthless, even when playing Monopoly. He never made any enemies who might have resented or plotted against him, and one of his most typical pieces of advice was 'you cannot be too kind'. And he never escalated the American military presence in Vietnam. Mind you, Dad never passed a major piece of Civil Rights legislation either, which does even up the score a bit.

One of the most striking features of Caro's project is its deft navigation of the ethical swamps of Johnson's life, and the way in which it initiates the reader into this world. His LBJ is compellingly nasty, and at times repellent, but also impressive in his ambition and his accomplishment. Johnson was brought up in a difficult world, and the Southwest Texas State Teachers College was the summit of his education, so it is hard not to feel on his side as the well-heeled

Kennedys and their Harvard advisers sneer at him, or to cheer at the heroism with which he rose to an unprecedented challenge after the assassination in Dallas. Even readers who come to Caro knowing nothing of the intricacies of Senatorial procedure in the middle years of the twentieth century (and I was certainly one of them), should be prepared to be dazzled at Johnson's transformation of a moribund debating chamber, rendered sclerotic by the filibustering power of the southern Democrats and the ossification of established interests, into a genuinely functioning organ of government. Caro's is a portrait of a man in the round, grotesque in many of his aspects, but nevertheless a captivating protagonist.

The books themselves are also vivid works of history. And one of the reasons why they take so long to trace his childhood, boyhood, youth and slow rise to the Senate, is the long contextual digressions that they take along the way. The chapter 'The Sad Irons' in *The Path to Power* describes the (sometimes literally) back-breaking domestic work of women in rural Texas before widespread electrification: the gallons of water drawn (and carried) by hand, the blistering work of washing, starching and ironing, or the preparation and preservation of food against the constant threat of starvation in a world that was on the edge. Caro thus provides the reader with a sense of the world that Johnson himself came from and also illustrates the transformative effect that the advent of affordable rural electrification had on this environment – a project for which Johnson was largely responsible.

The account of the Senatorial election of 1948 occupies much of *Means of Ascent* and is similarly a portrait of politics on the cusp of what we might regard as the modern political age: Johnson campaigned by helicopter, besmirched his opponent and stuffed ballot-boxes. And I would never have thought that the sub-committees and back-room deals of the mid-century Senate could possibly be interesting, until I read the third volume in the sequence. It might be a stretch to frame *Master of the Senate* alongside *The West Wing*, but the results are no less gripping.

None of this explains, of course, why I found *The Years of Lyndon Johnson* to be so comforting in a time of grief, and in truth it was only midway through Caro's sequence that I started to make sense of this myself. One thing lots of people say at funerals, of course, is how multiple people are buried there. There was the man I knew and loved, to be sure – a father, friend and adviser. But also the same person from different perspectives: a loving husband of half a century, grandfather, brother, colleague, teacher, friend. I was aware of many of these personas, of course, and had seen Dad play those roles while he was alive, but others were less expected, and were all the more pleasing for that. Former colleagues at the university spoke warmly of my father's teaching and his writing, his willingness to spend time with others and his readiness with a joke. All of this more or less fitted my image of my father, but it was still a surprise to hear of these many unexpected perspectives on an individual who was otherwise so familiar. Again, Johnson was nothing like Dad, but reading Caro's study did encourage reflection on the multiplicity of all of us, and on the complexity of the human experience.

The Years of Lyndon Johnson forms a living testimony to a life well-lived, but it is the biographer, and not his subject, for whom this will provide the most lasting monument, at least in the eyes of this grateful reader. At the time of writing, Robert Caro is apparently working on the fifth volume, almost half a century after embarking upon the first research for *The Path to Power*. The detail and density of his research, the hours spent in the Johnson archive, in libraries across the United States, or criss-crossing the Texas hill country, are apparent in every page of the work, and are overshadowed only by the vibrancy of his prose. This is writing to be savoured, each page a delight. And the accumulation of more than 3,000 of these pages, each the product of weeks of work, creates an impression that is almost sublime in its intensity. The books tell the story of a driven man, who changed the American world through sheer force of will, but there are two lives bound up in them, and both are extraordinary.

Ultimately, of course, I think four volumes of *The Years of Lyndon Johnson* were a salve for grief in part because they are so long. I finally finished *The Passage of Power* about four months after I had started the first volume (my reading was tempered with draughts of Margery Allingham and P. G. Wodehouse; even the most assiduous reader needs to offset intense political biography from time to time). By then another season had come and gone without Dad, and we were around the anniversary of his death. It was time passing, of course, that made the biggest difference, blunting the sharp pain of grief: the Caro books are great, but they aren't a panacea. Still, in their twinned portraits of lives well lived, they do offer a marvellous and engrossing place to hide for a few months.

ANDY MERRILLS lives in Leicester and is eagerly awaiting Volume 5 of the Caro biography. He teaches ancient history and is currently writing a book about a forgotten Latin epic.

The Nightmare of Room 101

CHRISTOPHER RUSH

It was a bright cold day in April and the clocks were striking thirteen.

That first arresting sentence of Orwell's *Nineteen Eighty-Four* transports us immediately into a world that is real enough (the swirl of gritty dust, the acidic sickly gin, the smell of boiled cabbage) but is also alien and fantastic. Even now, in the age of the 24-hour clock, that number thirteen startles you, for no clock ever does physically strike thirteen, and its undercurrent of unluckiness adds to the sense of unease. It's one of the best opening sentences I've ever read.

I have to confess that it was not the opening sentence that first gripped me. I never actually read it – because my first encounter with *Nineteen Eighty-Four* occurred when I was 10, too young a reader for the book that had been published, to an eruption of critical acclaim, by Secker & Warburg five years previously, in June 1949; but not too young a viewer to watch a young Peter Cushing play Winston Smith in the BBC's dramatization of Orwell's novel in 1954. That was the year in which a 12-inch black-and-white Bush TV set was wheeled in all its glory into our living-room, and so it was Orwell on the box that turned out to be my first experience of a classic work of world literature.

The year of the title, especially to a 10-year-old, seemed impossibly far off. It was science fiction. But Orwell's genius lay in making

George Orwell, *Nineteen Eighty-Four* (1949)
Penguin · Pb · 384pp · £8.99 · ISBN 9780141187761

fantasy seem real, and the images haunted me from that night on, the nightmares reaching a climax in memories of Room 101 and the terrifying spectacle of a mind broken on the wheel of its own worst fear: rats. I had an equivalent worst fear: crabs, and the terror of being eaten alive by them, stemming from my deep-sea-fisherman grandfather's stories of the crabs that dined sweetly on shipwrecked sailors. So I identified easily with Winston's rats, a direct importation into the novel of Orwell's own pathological fear, and of the punishment actually inflicted at one time on deserters from Teutonic armies; a rat was placed on the victim's stomach, trapped in a container, which was then heated to an unbearable degree, so that the rat's only exit from the micro-inferno was to rip into the man's stomach and eat its way out. Soul-blenching and sanguinary stuff. Critics who object that Orwell's cage-mask with its starving rats is a stagey device (it is to be attached to Winston's face, leaving eyes and cheeks accessible to the appetites of the ravenous rodents) would do well to remember this terrible form of punishment.

What *is* the novel – prophecy, propaganda, protest literature? I always taught my pupils that highly didactic one-sided writing cannot be great literature because in the greatest literature there is an authorial suspension of judgement and a textual ambivalence, a richness of meaning which outsoars the crudities of propaganda. Orwell is the one writer who broke the mould for me and produced a deeply instructive novel that is nonetheless a literary masterpiece.

He achieved this partly through the sheer vividness and realism of the writing. Far from being invented fantasy, much of it was painfully real to him. Winston's dream of a Golden Country is rooted in the paradise lost of Orwell's early childhood, the Edwardian Eden of Henley-on-Thames. Both author and protagonist combed junk shops for relics of the past, particularly glass paperweights with pictures enclosed, striking them with their fragile beauty, sealed off from the drab brutal reality of the world around them.

Orwell knew all about the brutality of controllers and tormentors from the bullies of his schooldays, just as he knew about large-scale authoritarianism from his time in India and Spain, and about the awfulness of power for power's sake, whether fascist or communist, and epitomised in the image of a boot crashing into a helpless human face. This is not so much a Wellsian warning as a shock tactic intended to startle readers into an awareness of present, not future dangers. After all 1984 is really 1948, when Orwell was still writing his novel and the fall of fascism had been followed by the rise of communism, so that the book's numerically inverted title projects the author's present despair on to a future world of dystopian science fiction. In it the main character, Winston Smith, is 'The Last Man in Europe' (the novel's originally intended title) to make a stand against state control: it is when his hopelessly doomed little rebellion is crushed that we are left feeling that humankind as we know it has been wiped out.

It's practically foretold for him in the choice of his name, which is an oxymoron, the first name reminding you of a leader who faced and overcame overwhelming odds, the surname anti-climactic and ordinary. Smith works in the Ministry of Truth in 'Airstrip One' (Britain renamed), part of the superstate Oceania, and his job is to re-document history to suit the needs of the all-powerful ruling Party, which also employs Thought Police to spy on those guilty of thought-crime and anti-state activities. The head of this state is Big Brother who, like God, is never seen but whose pictures and propaganda are everywhere. He demands total obedience to the Party and the subjugation of the individual.

Winston secretly rebels, dreaming of a pastoral idyll (the Golden Country), visiting junk shops and indulging in fantasies: that one day the proles might rise up and defeat the Party; and that in the meantime he might arrange a secret affair with a girl called Julia to whom he is attracted, in spite of his suspicion that she too may be one of the Thought Police. Orwell ensures that we wonder about that too. But they begin their affair and conduct it in a room above one of the junk shops, where they also plot against the Party, encouraged by an apparent dissident called O'Brien, who belongs to a group of underground activists, known as the Brotherhood. Or so they are led to believe.

Naturally they are arrested, beaten and imprisoned, tortured and retrained, prior to execution. It is when Winston still shows affection for his lost Julia that O'Brien sends him to Room 101, where he is told what awaits him: the rats. This is the cracking point when he screams: 'Do it to Julia! Do it to Julia! Not me! Julia! . . .' This is meant to shock and it does, and this is what the whole novel has led to. Everything we aspire to is doomed. Orwell makes you feel his own despair in your bones, as you do with Greek or Elizabethan heroes. Winston is a plaything of O'Brien's – the mouse to the cat, Raskolnikov to Porphyry, Faustus to Mephistopheles.

Orwell's union card, dated 29 December 1943

It's a bleak picture but not without beauty. For me one of the most powerful symbols of doomed hope occurs early in the novel. Winston has bought an ancient unused diary and prepares to write in it. The beautiful blank creamy pages are unsullied by a single syllable, like pristine snow. It is the author's moment of truth. It is also a form of thought-crime, punishable by death. What Winston does in fact write starts with the trivial and ends in drivel. And yet the diary is a symbol of the ultimate challenge to us, its blank pages our opportunity to speak to posterity, the tabula rasa for potentially the greatest book in the world.

An equally powerful symbol is the room above the junk shop. In it is a print of St Clement Danes, which revives memories of the old nursery rhyme 'Oranges and lemons,/Say the bells of St Clement's'. It sounds charmingly innocent and nostalgic but there is a sinister ending to it: 'Here comes a candle to light you to bed,/And here comes a chopper to chop off your head!'

The hidden threat is made real at the moment the lovers are addressed by a voice – 'You are the dead' – that echoes the words they have just spoken, perhaps the most chillingly heart-stopping moment in the book, and they realize that the print of the lovely vanished past has been used to conceal a telescreen, the terrible present lurking less than an inch away. In the same scene the paperweight is smashed. Innocence is illusory, beauty a broken dream. Only the Thought Police are real. And they burst into the room and the beating begins.

One other thing, on the subject of doomed beauty. When you think of the world's great stories of ill-fated love – Tristan and Isolde, Antony and Cleopatra – *Nineteen Eighty-Four* would be the last such classic to come to mind. But it not only contains a love story, it *is* a love story, and though the lovers may be a far cry from romantic star-crossed lovers, faithful unto death, they face their own malignant stars in the machinery of the totalitarian state which crushes them; but not before they have experienced the joy of sex as a liberation from that external control, and an assertion of their own vitality and mutual identity in the face of all the Party's efforts to destroy love.

But the most awful aspect of Orwell's love story is that the lovers are not only thwarted by the state – in the end they betray each other, to save their own skins. And it is at this point that we understand that this is not simply the story of one doomed love-affair, it is the story of the destruction of love itself. Even Philip Larkin famously offered an alternative to his pessimism with the line 'What will survive of us is love'. Orwell's message is bleak by comparison. Love will not survive us. What will survive is a terrible and terrifying travesty of love. The last line of the novel reinforces it: 'He loved Big Brother.'

Now that 1984 has passed and Eastern European communism has gone, does that date the novel and dim its relevance? It's clear to me that in 2020, seventy-odd years after it was first published, anyone looking at the map of the world will find all too many places where state control is alive and well. Far from being dated, Orwell's message is as relevant as ever. This is not a book restricted to 1948 or 1984 or any other year: it is a book about the human condition. And wherever there are individual men and women who wish to think for themselves and honour their own beliefs, and be free to do so without fear, Orwell's book will always make a timeless statement on their behalf. To think for yourself and not be brutalized or hanged or shot or beheaded for it – that is the eloquent plea of *Nineteen Eighty-Four*, a plea that needs to be heard now more than ever.

CHRISTOHER RUSH has always had a fondness for 1984, for that was the year in which he wrote his first book, *A Twelvemonth and a Day*, now listed as one of the 100 Best Scottish Books of All Time.

Murder and Walnut Cake

JULIE WELCH

For my son Tom. Since it was a vain attempt to match his prodigious literary output that got me into this situation in the
first place.

This slightly gushy (and therefore untypical) dedication at the front
of *Mrs Malory Wonders Why* was the first clue I had as to how and
why Hazel Holt created Sheila Malory. Thank goodness she did. Her
stories about a middle-aged widow who solves murder mysteries saw
me through a month in 2017 when two of my sons, simultaneously
and both on the other side of the world, were seriously ill. Similarly,
in March 2020 when it became clear that a pandemic was unavoid-
able and we had better hunker down or perish, I hunted out my store
of Mrs Malories again. Everyone has an author whose work they turn
to when it seems like the end of the world as we know it, and Hazel
Holt is mine. She is something of a mystery herself, though.

The twenty-one-book series can't be easily classified. The cover
blurbs of the American mass-market paperbacks that form the bulk
of my collection refer to Mrs Malory as a sleuth, conjuring up images
of a hardboiled character patrolling the mean streets of downtown
LA in a grubby raincoat, rather than a comfortably off grandmother
who wears tweed skirts and lives in a thatched cottage on the edge of
a small English seaside town.

Her best friend's daughter is a police inspector who frequently has

---

Many of Hazel Holt's Mrs Malory books are available in paperback from
Coffeetown Press and Allison & Busby.

Mrs Malory helping with enquiries, in a non-euphemistic sense. But the books are hardly crime thrillers. There is neither sex nor violence, only a corpse and the intensely curious Mrs Malory, with her beady eye for detail and instinct for what makes people tick, working out whodunnit. 'It's the way I feel about people, from my own knowledge of them, that makes me able to investigate them . . . You'd be surprised what you can find out from a little idle chat.' The goriest passages tend to be when Mrs M is cutting up ox heart for her dogs.

The books were published between 1989 and 2014, and by the end Mrs Malory is using the Internet and photographing the tyre tracks of a suspect on her smartphone, but all seem redolent of an earlier, gentler age. Set mainly in the fictional town of Taviscombe on the Somerset coast, hers is a world where there are still haberdashery counters, a Woolworths and 'a proper ironmonger's where men in brown overalls will still sell you half a dozen screws'. It reminds me of my own small-town childhood, which is probably why I find the books such soothing reading.

Sheila Malory meets her best friend Rosemary for lunch at The Buttery and hears of the latest enormities committed by Mrs Dudley, Rosemary's amusingly vicious gorgon of a mother. She endures committee meetings at which inevitably she is suckered into manning a stall at the Christmas Fayre or providing a cake for a Red Cross fête. She watches *Coronation Street* and pots up plants for the Help the Aged coffee morning, in between walking her dogs and tidying up after her disruptive Siamese cat. An Oxford graduate, she describes herself as being on the dustier fringes of the academic world. Her specialism is Victorian woman novelists; she often has a review to tackle for a literary magazine (typing a fierce condemnation of yet another study of Charlotte Brontë). She is always doing things 'briskly'. No wonder.

Within that structure, though, starkly modern issues are treated: paedophilia, coercive control, gay children rejected by their parents, old people left to dwindle in care homes. The latter provide the plot for mystery no. 3 in the series, *The Shortest Journey*, featuring Mrs Rossiter, a sweet, very rich widow, once bullied by her late husband and now bullied by her rapacious daughter – 'one of those small, slim, energetic women who make me feel like a large, ponderous, slow-thinking provincial'. It's a *The Lady Vanishes* tale with a wonderful somersault of an ending, and a narrative bound together, as are the others, by those descriptions of Mrs Malory's day-to-day life.

Comfort food plays a large part: home-made jam from a glut of plums, 'a rather good steamed chocolate sponge' with which she feeds an unwelcome visitor, the soon-to-be victim in *The Only Good Lawyer* . . . (no. 8). In *Death of a Dean* (no. 7), afternoon tea in the cathedral (shortbread, walnut cake and coffee éclairs) is the scene of a murder for which Mrs Malory's actor friend, David Beaumont, is the suspect.

But what about Mrs Malory's creator? Hazel Holt is best known as the biographer of Barbara Pym, whom she met in London in 1950 when both worked at the International African Institute in Fetter Lane. Holt was 22 and just out of Newnham College, Cambridge. She was Pym's friend and ally for twenty-five years, 'for much of that time sharing a small office with her, editing monographs, seminar studies and articles and reviews for the Institute's journal *Africa*'. Pym taught her the craft of editing and infected her with the bug of finding out about the people they encountered. Lunchtimes, when they weren't enjoying liver and bacon at the Lyons self-service restaurant in nearby Fleet Street, were 'spent in public libraries, searching for clues in *Crockford's*, Kelly's Directories or street maps'. All this reminded me of Dulcie Mainwaring and Viola Dace hunting for details about Aylwin Forbes in Pym's *No Fond Return of Love*.

Thirty years of close friendship ended with Pym's death in 1980, after which Holt set about selecting and editing her diaries and letters with the help of Pym's sister Hilary, for *A Very Private Eye* (1984), before producing the biography, *A Lot to Ask* (1990). As Pym's literary executor she also prepared four previously unloved novels for publication, including *An Unsuitable Attachment*, the rejection of which by her publisher had precipitated Pym into fourteen barren years.

What a frustrating job it was, though, to find out about Holt's life beyond her connection with Pym. Even Dulcie and Viola would have found the going tough. The American paperbacks offer a stock photo of her on a garden seat wearing a plain shirtwaister and sunglasses. She is reading the *Sunday Telegraph*, with her head turned aside as if reluctant to be photographed, even by her son Tom. A short entry on Wikipedia reveals that she was born on 3 September 1928, married Geoffrey Holt in 1951, and didn't start writing the Mrs Malories till she was in her sixties. As a girl, she had attended King Edward VI High School in Edgbaston, Birmingham. That rang a bell. I looked out *Delay of Execution*, no. 11 in the series, in which Mrs Malory spends a term at a girls' public day school, in Birmingham, as a temporary English teacher after the death of a Jean Brodie type. The dedication is 'For Barbara, Mary and Margaret, And all the rest of form 3c'. The school, with its plethora of new buildings among the 'old, original Victorian structure', is clearly modelled on Holt's own; I took a look at King Edward VI's website. The elusive Mrs Holt does not figure among the list of Notable Former Pupils.

Reduced to tracking the rest of her progress through life via the cover blurbs, I found more snippets of information. *The Only Good Lawyer* . . . disclosed that she was 'a former television reviewer and feature writer for *Stage and Television Today*', and that 'she now lives in Somerset with her husband, who is retired, and her cat'.

A little more information came to light in *The Silent Killer* (no. 15), where it was divulged that she 'currently lives on the edge of Exmoor, near Minehead, with her husband. Her life is divided between writing, cooking and trying to keep up with her Siamese cat, Flip.' I was amused that the cat now had a name, but the husband remained anonymous. By *Death Is a Word* (no. 21) her husband is not mentioned; it's just her and the Siamese cat.

How much of her own life experience went into the novels? In *The*

Cruellest Month, the second in the series, Mrs Malory returns to Oxford, where a suspicious death in the Bodleian takes her back into her own student past and the ecstasies and delusions of first love. I thought it might be autobiographical, but it is a young Barbara Pym, described as 'extrovert, full of naïve enthusiasms' in *A Lot to Ask*, who comes to mind. *The Cruellest Month*, incidentally, was the book she most enjoyed writing: while researching it she was given tours of the Bodleian by a helpful librarian and saw the subterranean bookstore which few civilians are able to penetrate. She used it to provide part of the solution to the murder.

The plot of *Fatal Legacy* (no. 10) also contains echoes of that thirty-year friendship. Sheila Malory is involved in a murder case when she learns that she has been appointed as literary executor to an old friend who has died suddenly. Any other similarities? There is the Siamese cat. She has a son, Michael, who throughout the books progresses from Oxford to the College of Law, marries, settles in Taviscombe and provides grandchildren. Tom Holt trained as a lawyer, too, though he gave it up after a few years to become a prolific sci-fi writer.

If only she had been more egotistic. After she died in 2015, posts on an online blog were testament to her popularity. Some, like me, had read the Mrs Malories multiple times. A bishop commented that he had discovered her work through membership of the Barbara Pym Society, and they had enjoyed a correspondence. Someone else lamented that no obituary had appeared in any of the British papers: 'I expected to see something in the *Guardian* at least,' one complained. I hope this piece will be some compensation.

JULIE WELCH was the first woman to report on football for a national newspaper, the *Observer*, and is the author of eleven books. Her latest is *The Fleet Street Girls*, which tells the story of the trail-blazing young women who entered the male-dominated world of journalism in the 1970s and 1980s.

Torrington's Tours

ROGER HUDSON

The Great North Road, the A1, bypasses the villages that used to punctuate it and so misses out on the inns where John Byng, Lord Torrington, regularly used to stay on his touring holidays during the 1780s and '90s. I have driven along it from London to Newark and back again far too often and am grateful to him for helping me relieve the boredom by recalling his experiences at the Sun in Biggleswade, the George at Buckden (good cream there, and a political barber), the Wheatsheaf on Alconbury Hill, or the Haycock on the Nene at Wandsford. They are recorded in the travel journals of this retired Colonel of the Foot Guards – he was only the 5th Viscount Torrington for the last few weeks of his life after his elder brother died in 1812 without an heir.

The Byngs came to prominence as a naval family, the 1st Viscount wisely backing William of Orange in 1688, and his career culminating in his crushing defeat of the Spanish fleet at Cape Passaro in 1718. His third son, another admiral, was less fortunate, ending up before a firing squad on his own quarterdeck after a court martial for his failure against the French at Minorca in 1757. His nephew the diarist (b. 1742) was already being 'train'd up to glory', as a page of honour to George II, before becoming a cornet in the Royal Horse Guards in 1760, transferring to the Foot Guards in 1762. He married in 1767 and although this resulted in thirteen children it seems he was

John Byng's diaries first appeared in four volumes between 1934 and 1938. A one-volume abridged edition came out in 1954, and the Folio Society published a selection entitled *Rides Round Britain* in 1996.

cuckolded by his friend William Windham of Felbrigg Hall in Norfolk. Another major misfortune was his involvement in his elder brother's financial collapse in 1777, which led to them both having to flee to the Continent to escape their creditors. Byng left the army in 1780 for a post in the Stamp Office, part of the Inland Revenue located in the newly built Somerset House, where he worked until 1799.

For a man whose greatest pleasure early in life was hunting, having to live in London with one's marriage under strain, a house near Manchester Square full to bursting with children, and a tedious job was a trial, and the need to escape obvious: 'not to be worried every morning by revenue prosecutions and every evening by sights and relations of follies and fashions . . . the eternal raps at my door, with the never-ending admission of milliners (who must be followed up by bills)'. This was why he yearned for 'the passage through a new country, upon a safe horse, in a charming summer morning . . . to rummage myself forth, to observe and descant upon my own country'. That was the way to restore his strength so he could again face his wife, 'a complainant who refines upon pleasure until it becomes a pain'.

Although they must have allowed him to cover much more ground, Byng disliked the new network of turnpike roads, because 'they have imported London manners and depopulated the country. I meet milkmaids on the road with the dress and looks of Strand misses.' What's more, while their curved surface made them drain well and enabled a post-chaise to travel at speed, they were hard, stony and dusty, making riding much worse than on the old tracks. He also hated the enclosures with their hedges and fences which denied him 'excellent scampering over downs, heaths and commons'.

He nearly always seemed to travel with a manservant and sometimes a dog but did not want the former's company when riding: 'I detached him forward to prepare for me and my horses, proper accommodations at night. That is the true use of servants on the road' – and the way to avoid dirty glasses, ill-made beds and horses left in the care of drunken, roguish ostlers. 'As for my sheets, I always take them with me', for he knew that those on the inn beds would probably be dirty or damp, or both. The servant took the baggage, except for a cloak bag containing a night cap and great coat, which Byng had behind him on his horse. If the blankets smelt, he sprinkled brandy on them. If wet through, he washed himself in brandy. It probably would have been smuggled – he twice passed well-mounted gangs of smugglers on his travels near the south coast.

For shaving he used a barber if there was one, but he was also complimented on his ability to shave himself. If there was a bookshop nearby he always visited it, and he was always disappointed in what he found; he was an avid reader of newspapers, noting that the London evening papers arrived in Leicester by ten the next morning. Before he set out he must have left a list of places to which letters should be sent for him to collect. Writing answers to them, keeping up his diary and sticking in it the bills from the inns where he had stayed occupied him after supper. The normal time for dinner was four o'clock, and he far preferred to serve himself from a dumb waiter and not to be waited on 'by a nasty, dirty wench, watching you all the time, picking her nails, blowing her nose upon her apron, and then wiping the knives and glasses with it, or spitting and blowing on the plates'. Before and often after dinner he went for a walk, and if there was an interesting building, then he often did a sketch of it. But he mostly had to find them for himself, because ostlers, waiters and landlords were quite ignorant of such things, as they were of the way to anywhere.

He was very keen on an early start: 'I call for the bill in the night before my departure; rise early; eat a slice of bread and butter and drink some milk that I took upstairs with me; then ride ten miles to breakfast; there shirt and shave; by which means I get a forward day, and my horse baits while I dress.' His guiding principle on the tour was that 'we came to see, and not to shrink from idleness, or imaginary civility'. Thus he was quite prepared to go to a door, ring the bell and ask to see the house, relying on his obvious gentry status to gain him entry.

A repeated debate he had with himself was on the pros and cons of travelling alone. He disliked having to fall in with his companions' ways, but the lone tourist 'requires vigour of mind and of body, else he droops'. If the weather was bad it made the problem worse: 'What can exceed the dullness of a country town on a Sunday evening in a heavy rain?' The universal system at inns was to charge only for food and drink. For Byng, 'The obligation at an inn forces me to eat meats and swallow spirituous liquors of every bad quality.' But quite often the food was acceptable enough: fresh-caught salmon and good perry at Worcester, an excellent pigeon pie with a pint of port, 'a fowl kill'd in honour of our arrival, with a large quantity of beef steaks, flank'd by a stack of asparagus, each one foot in height, satisfied me'.

The latter part of the eighteenth century saw a new enthusiasm for old buildings, valued for the associations they summoned up, the stimulus they gave to the imagination. This, the Picturesque approach, was very much Byng's as he sought out ruined abbeys, monastic remains, cathedrals, castles, half-timbered houses and old 'gentleman's seats', preferably of stone and still with casement, not sash windows, and elaborate chimneypieces. In churches he was always on the lookout for holy water stoups, fonts and stained glass; if he ever saw a glazier's shop he went in, in hopes of finding some. He wanted ruins 'clear'd from adjoining buildings and fenced around, with a lodge of entrance, the ivy to be spread around, trees to spring up'. Among his favourite abbeys were Tintern, Fountains and Egglestone by Barnard Castle, the furthest north he got. Southwell Minster delighted him and Lincoln Cathedral he far preferred to St Paul's, though he was saddened by its sparse congregation. His trip to North Wales allowed him to run the gamut of Edward I's great castles there, clamber up to a succession of dramatic waterfalls, and hire the local harpists to play. Hardwick Hall he called 'the foremost old manor I ever saw'. At Warwick Castle he was 'enwrapt in the chaemeras of chivalry'.

These were his loves of which he went in search. But he was a good hater too: of new red brick, of bow windows, of the 'Adamatic' fashion – Robert Adams's neoclassical style – of new French furniture; of too 'sprucified' parks and those who cut down their avenues of oak and replaced them with mean clumps of Scots pine, larches or Lombardy poplars; of mountain tops, since 'All wide views are horrors to me – like an embarkment into Eternity.' A paternalist through and through, he deplored the absentee gentry, removed from the country by what he called 'this London suction', because without them where was the 'justice, example, charity, every help and every succour' on which poor villagers relied? He blamed enclosures for depopulating the countryside and for depriving the cottagers of their large gardens, pasturage and firewood. 'On *my* estate, there shall be no mud cottages, and my comfortable cottagers shall be obliged to have land, and to be happy.'

He pointed out that those in Manchester most vociferous against the slave trade were those who imported bands of orphan children from London to work in the mills. Yet of the new Sunday schools, he said he was 'point blank against these institutions; the poor should not read, and of writing I never heard, for them, the use'. As for religion, 'I find it to be lodged in the hands of the Methodists, men most commendable and useful to the nation, as the greater clergy do not attend their duty and the lesser neglect it.'

His wish, most of the time, was that 'trade was unknown', since 'it leads to commerce, commerce leads to war and war brings taxes'. The true concern of 'this island of interior happiness' was the landed property, which he contrasted with what he saw, for instance, in Stockport: 'drunken weavers led home by their soberer comrades, men and children killed by gin, a weaver's body hanged in chains for murder of his wife'. But on his first visit to Cromford he was impressed by Sir Richard Arkwright's 'three magnificent cotton mills', feeling he had 'honourably made his great fortune', and he could write when at Leicester of 'the prosperous cotton trade which populates and enriches all the neighbouring counties'. In 1794, when he heard the news of the naval victory over the French known as the Glorious First of June, he paid for the Biggleswade bells to be rung in celebration, though a few days before he had been condemning the war as 'hastily and unthinkingly plunged into'.

Byng may have said his habits and thoughts had become 'fixed like rusty weathercocks or like matrimony, for better or worse', but we are still indebted to his wish 'to lounge about the country in search of Antiquity and the Beauties of Nature', and his urge to record it all, even when 'rains and glooms quite despond the tourist' and he rather wishes himself in a London drawing-room or coffee house. How else to know that, going out to take 'a peep at the moon', he 'was not displeased to hear the skuttling of lovers; most comfortable in the Summer for the poor, who come forth with the butterfly for a little buzz', or that one cold June the women haymakers were 'wrap't up, no loose stays, no fine, easy, sweaty dishevelment', or that when he went to a performance by some travelling players, there were only thirteen candles to light it, and one fiddle for music?

He loved 'to hear the squeak of a fiddle, and always look about for a cricket match or fives playing [against the walls and buttresses of the parish church], for little recreation have the poor, and but a short summer'. It is this fundamental humanity and his amused, observant eye, so often to be found in his turns of phrase, that make him such a good companion through the English counties and the Welsh mountains.

ROGER HUDSON reckons he must have driven about 185,000 miles in the last fifty years or so, going from London to Newark and back again on the Great North Road. His *An Englishman's Commonplace Book* was published by Slightly Foxed last year.

For those who would like to read more about the diaries, Roger has supplied an appendix which can be found on our website: see www.foxedquarterly.com/roger-hudson-torrington-diaries.

Love at First Sight

CHARLES HEBBERT

At a loose end after university in the 1980s I went to Budapest to learn Hungarian. My teacher gave our group a Hungarian novel from which we studied passages in class. It was a slim book with an enticing cover photograph of the Bridge of Sighs and an intriguing title: *Utas és holdvilág* – literally, 'Traveller and Moonlight'.

The opening line lures you in: 'On the train, everything seemed fine. The trouble began in Venice, with the back-alleys.' Mihály and Erzsi are two young Hungarians on their honeymoon in Italy. In Venice Mihály goes off on his own one evening and gets lost in the back-alleys. He is looking for a drink, but even he is not quite sure what kind of drink – which sets the tone for his journey through the book.

The couple then move on to Ravenna: 'The place smells like a corpse, Ravenna's a decadent city,' says Mihály. He and Erzsi are sitting in the main square when a motorbike roars towards them and an old classmate of Mihály's jumps off. After an awkward exchange the man, a rogue with the satisfying name of János Szepetneki, who has studiously ignored Erzsi, declares: 'I'm going. Your wife, by the way, is a thoroughly repulsive woman.' This brutal comment about Erzsi, a 'well-dressed, attractive woman', leads to Mihály telling her

Translations by Len Rix of Antal Szerb's *The Third Tower* (1936), *Journey by Moonlight* (1937) and *Oliver VII* (1943) are all available in paperback from Pushkin Press. A collection of Szerb's literary essays, *Reflections in the Library*, on Blake, Milton, Gogol and other writers, has been translated by Peter Sherwood (Legenda, 2016).

all about his wild childhood friends, whose shadows fall across the length of the book.

By now I was hooked, and avidly read the rest of the book on my own. However, my thirst to find out what happened outstripped my limited knowledge of the language, so though I raced through the book, enjoying its flow, I missed much of the detail.

Fast forward twenty years, when I read Nicholas Lezard's ecstatic review in the *Guardian* of a new translation by Len Rix of *Utas és holdvilág*, translated as *Journey by Moonlight*. Opening the book was like returning to a conversation with an old friend. I was transported back to the feelings I had had when I first read it, but now I discovered the nuances that had escaped me before.

This was the beginning of my renewed love affair with Antal Szerb, fuelled by successive translations of his works by Rix. When I met the translator a year or so later, he told me he had also learnt the language with the help of this book, though in his case he had pursued his learning rather further.

Rix had already been intrigued by the sound of spoken Hungarian when he was given the novel by Hungarian friends. 'This is the book we all read as students,' they said. It was love at first sight. He decided to teach himself Hungarian, which in turn led to a translation. This he assiduously worked on for six or seven years, masterfully polishing it into its final state.

Szerb would surely have been delighted that he had been 'found' by such a kindred spirit. Like Szerb, Rix was a teacher until he retired and is fascinated by languages; and beneath a quiet humility burns a strong passion that becomes apparent when he talks about Szerb and other writers he has translated.

Journey by Moonlight certainly deserves to be more widely known. Its very unheroic hero Mihály is finally settling down after years of being a bit of a wastrel: he has 'married well' and is going to take his position in the family firm. 'It was Mihály's first visit to Italy at the age of thirty-six, on his honeymoon.' He had always been afraid of

Italy, which he 'associated with grown-up matters'. But now that he was married, Italy was no longer a danger.

However, Italy unravels his respectability and awakens in him a nostalgia for his lost friends and their bohemian life. As he goes down more and more blind alleys, Mihály misjudges both himself and those around him at every turn.

A kind and modest man himself, Szerb presents even the humiliation of his hero in a very human way, not least because Mihály's struggle with the questions of self and identity had roots deep in Szerb's own life. Born in 1901, Antal Szerb grew up in the complex world of an assimilated Jewish family in Budapest. When he was a child his parents became Catholics – Hungary was noted for encouraging its Jewish population to convert. Indeed, Jews felt more secure there than elsewhere in the region, so much so that even in the late 1930s Szerb and many others did not take the chance to escape: Hungary is our home, they said, we won't be harmed here. Szerb went to a good Catholic school and joined the Boy Scouts, but his early writings show that amid the growing undercurrents of nationalism the question was always there: where did he belong?

He toyed with the idea of becoming a priest but instead became a teacher, reading and writing feverishly in his spare time. He also travelled to Paris and lived for a year in London in 1929–30. A keen Anglophile, he spent much of his time there in the old British Library Reading Room, falling in love with English literature and translating writers such as P. G. Wodehouse.

In 1934 he found his writing voice, completing his *History of Hungarian Literature* and his first novel, *The Pendragon Legend*, a comic masterpiece of murder, mystery and misguidedness set in England and Wales. Both books displayed his vast breadth of reading – in the latter he included numerous parodies of English authors – and both were a great success.

In 1937 came *Journey by Moonlight*, which became a cult book after the war and is his best-known work. However, as Hungary tied its future to Hitler and fascism, a succession of laws from 1938 onwards stole the property and then the freedom of those like Szerb who were now officially identified as Jewish.

While anti-Semitic feeling grew on the streets, Szerb continued to work at the same frenetic pace. Alongside his job teaching literature in an economics school (where he was revered by his pupils) he completed his *History of World Literature* in 1941 and his masterly novel *Oliver VII* and *The Queen's Necklace*, the true story of a fraud involving Marie Antoinette, in 1942. In 1943 he was thrown out of his teaching post and his books were banned (he tried to pass *Oliver* off as a translation from the English to get round the ban). Later that year the Hungarian fascists drafted him into forced labour close to Budapest.

In 1944 his labour unit, which included two close friends, both writers, was dispatched to western Hungary to work on the defences that were supposed to keep the advancing Soviets at bay, but the living conditions in the work camps were so horrendous that they amounted to little more than death camps. Nonetheless Szerb rejected the chance to escape, not wanting to abandon his friends. On the day that Auschwitz was liberated, 27 January 1945, a weakened Szerb was beaten to death by his guards, and his friends died soon after. With the murder or exile of so many Hungarian writers, artists and scientists, now classed as Jews, the country lost a generation of its finest talent.

Yet the defeat of the fascists brought no improvement in Szerb's literary standing in Hungary. For the fascists Szerb had been Jewish, not Hungarian, and nationalists had not liked the way he took the nation's great names off their pedestal and wrote about them with humour and gentle irony. For the post-war communist regime, however, he was too bourgeois, and his lack of appreciation for Soviet writers kept him out of favour.

Even today Hungarian literary scholars do not give Szerb the critical attention he deserves. The only full biography of the writer is notably unsympathetic and ignores *Oliver VII*, while even more supportive critics dismiss it as lightweight. In 1990 the authorities tried

to rename a school in Budapest that is named after him. The idea persists that he is somehow not patriotic enough. Szerb's short, simple sentences, influenced by his study of French and English, may be a translator's dream but they do not endear him to those Hungarians for whom only long tortuous sentences can be serious. As Szerb wrote in his introduction to *The Queen's Necklace*: 'People in this country expect scholarly works to be unreadable.' His work, of course, is quite the opposite.

Yet it is somehow fitting that Szerb's style poses these challenges: the difficulties in classifying his work mirror his own struggles with the questions of who he was and where he belonged, just as his heroes always struggle to see their way ahead.

Szerb described his own work as 'neo-frivolous', which captures very nicely the consciously self-ironic style that conceals more serious concerns. Critics who dismiss *Journey by Moonlight* as a decadent bourgeois novel or *Oliver VII* as a romp miss the essence of the man and his work. *Oliver VII* best epitomizes this misinterpretation. Here Szerb picks up his earlier themes: again a young man tries to find his way, uncertain of his path into adulthood. Yet while János Bátky blunders around blindly in *The Pendragon Legend* and Mihály in *Journey by Moonlight* faces humiliation and defeat, Oliver rises to the challenge. The hero – and this time he *is* a hero – is the newly crowned king of a small central European state who doesn't want to be king. He secretly organizes a coup against himself and disappears, landing in the company of some con men. When he ends up having to pretend to be himself, King Oliver VII, he understands, albeit reluctantly, that he must actively embrace his fate. Unlike the earlier novels, here the ending is hopeful, with a sense of loose ends being tied up – an extraordinary book given the circumstances in which he wrote it.

An insight into this fascinating writer can be found in his account of a trip to Italy in 1936. *The Third Tower* tells of how he travels round some of the places that would feature in his works, such as Venice and Ravenna, but is restless. Eventually he visits San Marino and finds himself alone, away from the hordes of tourists, by a tower that overlooks the tiny country. 'For the first time on my present journey I am happy . . . The happiness I feel here . . . is something I must not give up for anyone: anyone or anything. I cannot surrender my soul to any nation state or any set of beliefs.' He feels like a man for our times.

CHARLES HEBBERT is an editor and translator. He lived for ten years in Budapest and was a co-author of the *Rough Guide* to the city. As he plays his accordion, he dreams of translating other fine Hungarian writers from the 1930s.

Thank You, Dr Spock

ALICE JOLLY

A night in the autumn of 2002. I am woken by a scream which threatens to blow the chimneys off the house. I rush into the next room, pick up my 3-month-old son and do my best to comfort him. His tiny face is purple and he's thrashing and writhing in pain. My husband is away on a business trip. What can I do? I have no idea.

It's four in the morning and I'm tearful and exhausted. We're living in Brussels so we have no family to help us. Our tiny son, born prematurely, has colic, so over the past three months we've taken it in turns to spend half the night holding him in our arms as we pace up and down the bedroom. This scream, however, is not a colic scream. It is the worst scream I have ever heard. I can feel it in my jaw, my kidneys, the soles of my feet. Clearly my son is about to die and it will be my fault. I had never thought that being a mother would be easy but why had nobody told me that it might push me to the brink of insanity?

I was furious with myself for being so useless. I had won a scholarship to Oxford and written books. Other women seemed to manage perfectly well. Of course I could look after a baby – except I couldn't. Weeping, I took my son downstairs to make a hot-water bottle. Putting him in the pram, parked next to the bookcase, my eyes settled on a cheap yellow paperback with scuffed corners and brown pages. It was a book my mother had given me: *Baby and Child Care* by Dr Benjamin Spock.

Benjamin Spock, *Dr Spock's Baby and Child Care* (1946: 10th edition 2018)
Gallery Books · Pb · 992pp · £16.99 · ISBN 9781501175336

The sight of it made me angry. Why had she given me a book she'd used thirty years ago? But I pulled it down and it fell open at a well-thumbed page. In the case of an ear infection, I read, 'a baby may . . . cry piercingly for several hours'. Immediately the situation seemed manageable. I was only two miles from a hospital. I just had to get through the next three hours and then I would get my son to a doctor.

I filled the hot-water bottle and then dosed my yelling baby with a dangerous amount of Calpol, took several large swigs myself, and placed him on my chest. Too shaken to sleep, I began to read. And in that dewy dawn, alone in a foreign city, I found myself listening to a voice of kindness, calm and authority: 'You know more than you think you do.'

As my son recovered from his ear infection, I read more. *Baby and Child Care* was first published in 1946 (my 1963 copy was a 'new, extensively revised and enlarged version') so I expected to find it full of brisk certainty, but Dr Spock makes it clear that he doesn't have all the answers. 'The most important thing is that you should not take too literally what is said in this book.' Instead, you should trust yourself. 'What good mothers and fathers instinctively feel like doing for their babies is usually best after all,' he tells us. And, in fact, you don't even need to know what you instinctively want to do. All will be well 'as long as the mother acts as though she knows what she is doing'.

Dr Spock also tells us repeatedly that a baby cannot be contented if its mother is not happy. Describing a stressed mother (I recognized myself) he does suggest that a psychiatrist is sometimes needed, but first, he recommends, 'Go to a movie, or a beauty parlour, or get yourself a new hat or dress.' Clearly, my kind of childcare expert. He also discusses the need to embrace ambivalent parenting, with whole sections on 'Mixed feelings about pregnancy' and on how 'Love for the baby comes gradually'. And he is reassuring about the parent's right to feel angry. 'A natural, outspoken good mother whose child has been bedevilling her is able to say to a friend half-jokingly . . . "I'd enjoy giving him a thorough walloping."'

He tells us that it is entirely acceptable to find your child 'uncomfortable, baffling and challenging . . . Parents can't order what they want. They take what they get . . . Parents do the best they know how with the kind of child they receive.' He warns parents against setting themselves impossibly high standards or becoming confused with new theories. What is important is to stick to your convictions.

For Dr Spock a baby is both 'our creation . . . our visible immortality' and 'a reasonable and friendly human being'. However, the cheery little devil is also infinitely cunning and out to prevent you and your husband having any fun. Dr Spock is keen to tell you how to outwit the little devil. I was more than happy to sign up to his plan.

As well as being good on the psychology of family life, Dr Spock is also practical. His advice is often wonderfully homespun. You don't need a crib, 'a box or bureau drawer will do', and 'you can make a mattress by folding up an old blanket', though he does concede that, 'Now is the time to get an automatic washer or drier if you can possibly afford one.'

Baby and Child Care was written in an era when families in some parts of America were many miles from a doctor, and consequently first aid and home remedies are covered extensively. It explains how to build a homemade incubator and how to use a badminton net to stop a child from climbing out of a cot. Croup can be successfully treated by boiling a pan of water and putting an umbrella over your head while holding your baby in your arms near the pan so it can breathe the steam. While my husband and I laughed at these ideas, they also proved strengthening. They reminded me that, since the beginning of time, women have nursed their children through life-threatening illnesses with no outside help at all. Channelling the strength of those pioneer women gave me a new courage and certainty. I was back from the brink.

Three months later Dr Spock saved me again. I had breast-fed my son successfully up to that point and then suddenly it all went wrong. He just wouldn't feed. He'd suck a few times and then begin to cry.

This went on for days and then weeks. He cried and I cried. We were both exhausted. I spoke to other mothers and they were either dismissive or bossy. Breast-feeding is entirely natural, was the message: it works just fine. Maybe you need to relax and get some sleep. The medical profession was also of little help. Again, the implication was that I was not cut out for breast-feeding: all real women, real mothers, would find it natural and easy.

Dr Spock took a different view. In his book I found a detailed description of exactly what was happening. The problem was that my son was teething. Since he was tiny and premature everyone else had assumed that couldn't be the case, but I knew Dr Spock was right and bought a bottle and formula.

The militant, middle-class breast-feeders at the mother and baby groups were appalled. I didn't care and was angry I'd been misled by their near-religious zeal for breast-feeding. I was learning the value of my instinct. I had got my confidence back. Bottles and formula ensured that I was no longer exhausted and anaemic, and my son was no longer hungry. I had understood Dr Spock's most essential message: 'Every time you change him, bathe him, feed him, smile at him, he's getting a feeling that he belongs to you and that you belong to him. Nobody else in the world, no matter how skilful, can give that to him.' I was my son's mother and, therefore, I was the best mother he could have, no matter how inadequate my approach.

As a young man Benjamin Spock won a gold medal for rowing at the Paris Olympics. Seven new editions of his book were produced during his lifetime and another two after his death. According to the *New York Times*, in its first fifty-two years, it was the bestselling book after the Bible and it is still selling throughout the world. This huge success was bound to cause a backlash at some point and when, in the 1960s, Dr Spock was arrested while protesting against the Vietnam War, conservative America turned against him. He was accused of basing his advice on anecdotal evidence rather than academic research. And inevitably, as scientific knowledge advanced, some of his advice became outdated – for instance that babies should be put to sleep on their tummies rather than on their backs.

He was also held responsible for all the counter-cultural movements of the time. 'The Spock Generation' had been ruined by his permissive views. These arguments still persist, despite the fact that Dr Spock never championed permissive parenting. In fact, his views on that subject are as mild and flexible as on nearly every other: 'Good-hearted parents can get good results with either moderate strictness or moderate permissiveness.' In our modern age of intolerance and anxiety, his voice continues to sound out with real wisdom and gentleness. You'll get through, he seems to say.

We did get through. Our son has now turned 18 and is an infinitely reasonable and friendly human being. Thank you, Dr Spock, for offering words of encouragement during the dark days. I still think your book is of much more use than its many modern equivalents. It isn't just about being a parent, it is also about a certain attitude to life. It promotes the value of being open and honest, of accepting life's vagaries. If you approach things with a certain confidence, admit your failings and do your best, it tells us, then all will be well. And even if that isn't quite true, sometimes just believing it is enough to carry you through.

ALICE JOLLY's most recent novel *Mary Ann Sate, Imbecile* was runner-up for the Rathbones Folio Prize and was on the longlist for the Ondaatje Prize. She teaches creative writing at the University of Oxford.

Judgement Day

C. J. DRIVER

After a lifetime of teaching English literature, I have accumulated a private and rather eclectic pantheon of great (mainly modern) novels, in which J. L. Carr's *A Month in the Country* holds a central place. Carr finished it in 1978, and it was published in 1980 by the Harvester Press, and then by Penguin in paperback. The novel received more acclaim in America than in Britain, although it did make the shortlist for the Booker Prize, where it lost out to one of William Golding's less successful novels. In due course, as was Carr's wont – because he thought little of most commercial publishers – he bought back the rights and published it under his own imprint of the Quince Tree Press, from which (blessedly) copies are still available (as are Carr's seven other novels).

It is generally agreed that *A Month in the Country* is Carr's masterpiece, although it is a very short novel (E. M. Forster would have defined it as a novella): in the Quince Tree edition, 106 pages only. It is set in Yorkshire in 1920, in what was apparently a marvellous summer. The two central characters, Tom Birkin and Charles Moon, had been soldiers in the trenches of the Western Front. We discover, quite late on, that Moon had been found in bed with his batman, stripped of his captain's rank and sent to a military prison, despite a record of bravery which had won him the Military Cross. Birkin had been a 'forward signaller', sent out beyond the trenches to direct artil-

---

J. L. Carr, *A Month in the Country* (1980) can be ordered direct from the Quince Tree Press (Pb · 106pp · £9: www.quincetreepress.co.uk). There is also a Penguin edition available (Pb · 128pp · £7.99 · ISBN 9780141182308).

lery fire; very few of them survived for long. So both he and Moon know about Hell, though they call it Passchendaele.

Birkin (the first-person narrator of the novel) and Moon are benefiting from a legacy given by the late Miss Adelaide Hebron to the fabric fund of the Anglican parish church in the village of Oxgodby, in part to pay for Birkin, a trained restorer, to uncover a medieval wall-painting and for Moon, an archaeologist, to seek out the grave of one of Miss Hebron's ancestors, Piers, buried in the fourteenth century outside consecrated ground because he had been excommunicated.

Christopher Fiddes

Moon lives in a tent over a trench he has dug in a field next to the churchyard, and Birkin sets up lodgings in the bell-tower of the church. Moon has an informed notion of where he will find the grave of Miss Hebron's ancestor but he is more interested in what he thinks may be the relics of a much earlier building on the same site, while

Birkin spends his days dangerously up ladders and scaffolding, gradually uncovering what he realizes is a work of genius, an almost undamaged painting of the Judgement Day, though it has been covered over for four hundred years.

The two stories merge in the last pages of the novel: the 'falling man' in the painting who is going down into the fires of Hell is almost certainly a portrait of the man whose bones Moon (helped by Birkin) finds in the dust of his shroud. Moon and Birkin open the stone coffin and look at the skeleton: 'A metal thing swung from the rib-cage; [Moon] poked in a pencil and delicately fished it out. "Well, well, the crescent! So that was why they wouldn't let him into the church. He was a Muslim. Caught in some expedition and then became a convert to save his skin!"'

There is another theme, probably the moral centre of the novel: Birkin is married, but his wife has gone off with another man, as she has a habit of doing. Birkin is fairly sure that, while he was away at war, Vinny had slept with other men too; now he knows for sure that she is serially unfaithful. The vicar, the Reverend J. G. Keach, a difficult and awkward man, deeply unsuited to the Oxgodby community and too poor to enjoy the huge rectory in which he lives, has a beautiful wife called Alice who is much younger than him. Alice makes friends with Birkin, often coming to watch him at work, and he (lonely, damaged man) falls in love with her; but when the moment comes in which he might do something about that attraction he doesn't take the chance. They are in the bell-chamber, looking out to where Moon has been excavating:

She turned . . . so that her breasts were pressing against me. And, although we both looked outward across the meadow, she didn't draw away as quite easily she could have done.

I should have lifted an arm and taken her shoulder, turned her face and kissed her. It was that kind of day. It was why she'd come. Then everything would have been different. My life, hers. We would have had to speak and said aloud what both of us knew and then, maybe, turned from the window and lain down together on my makeshift bed. Afterwards, we would have gone away, maybe on the next train. My heart was racing. I was breathless. She leaned on me, waiting. And I did nothing and said nothing . . .

I am quite glad I never had to teach the novel, because I know how difficult it would have been to get Sixth Formers to understand that decision, although it is utterly in character. 'But why doesn't he take the chance? She wants him, doesn't she? They want each other, don't they?' I can see my good-hearted pupils frowning as they struggle to understand something so un-modern, a self-denial entirely atypical of the world in which most of us now live, where self-fulfilment, particularly of the sexual kind, has become our touchstone. Denial is unhealthy, isn't it?

It is only after that non-event that Vinny writes to Birkin to say she wants to return to him; and he knows he will accept her, even though she is certain to desert him yet again. When he goes to the rectory to say farewell, he finds the Keaches have packed up and left, probably for the more welcoming communities of Sussex. He will never see Alice again.

Rereading the novel for the umpteenth time, I was once again astonished at how much there is in such a short book. Birkin gets himself quite deeply involved in the local community, in particular making friends with the Ellerbeck family, stalwarts of local Methodism. He umpires cricket matches, helps with the harvesting, even one Sunday finds himself subbing for Mr Ellerbeck as preacher at a Methodist service. (There is a wonderfully happy account of a day's outing with the Chapel people.) Above all, there is a marvellous description of the great wall-painting of the Judgement Day which Birkin is employed to uncover. Carr was passionately committed to the preservation of old churches, as Byron Rogers recounts in *The*

Last Englishman: The Life of J. L. Carr (2003), and clearly had a degree of expertise about medieval wall-painting.

Birkin gradually realizes he is dealing with a masterpiece: 'A tremendous waterfall of colour, the blues of the apex falling, then seething into a turbulence of red; like all truly great works of art, hammering you with its whole before beguiling you with its parts . . .' Just before he leaves Oxgodby for ever, he goes to look at the painting again and knows that, 'whatever else had befallen me during those few weeks in the country, I had lived with a very great artist . . . And, standing before the great spread of colour, I felt the old tingling excitement and a sureness that the time would come when some stranger would stand there too and understand . . .'

If you care about novels, you should get hold of a copy of *A Month in the Country*. It is a great novel and will be read long after some of the detritus acclaimed these days has been flushed away by our blessed ally, Time.

C. J. (JONTY) DRIVER has written novels, memoirs, biographies and seven collections of poems, the latest of which is *Before* (2018). Another collection, *Still Further: New Poems, 2000–2019*, will be published by the Uhlanga Press this year.

Light in the Dark Ages

SUE GAISFORD

Nobody likes losing a pet. But for Owain it is the very last straw. His father and his older brother were killed in the last great battle against the invading Saxons, a battle which he himself barely survived; he gave up his own freedom and became enslaved, to save the life of a sick girl he had befriended; his country, his home and his own family have been either overrun or destroyed and now Dog, his only friend, has been cruelly, pointlessly killed. Who could blame him for feeling suicidal?

He makes for a place in the woods where, long ago, the Romans had made a shrine, now of course crumbling and overgrown. He buries Dog, and finds himself saying a prayer – not to the Christian god of his childhood, but to Silvanus, the old Roman deity of the woodlands. Then, crawling into the little shelter, he sits and idly scrapes away the leaves at his feet, uncovering a beautiful, delicate tiled floor, where a girl dressed in blue forever plays with tiny birds. And his spirits revive, and he resolves to live.

It is a pivotal moment. We loved Owain from the start, but now we cheer him on, trusting him to become the man he wants to be. And he doesn't fail us.

The sobering thing about this episode in Rosemary Sutcliff's *Dawn Wind* (1961) is that so little has changed. People still go to war, are still cruel to animals; slavery has never gone away – and discovering Roman remains is the daily work of 'detectorists'. But the fictional Owain lived more than fourteen hundred years ago, in a period which, having left precious few relics of its very existence, is known as the Dark Ages.

Charles Keeping

Nowadays, historians often prefer the term Early Middle Ages. But for those living through them, those years must often have felt very dark. In *Dawn Wind*, the fifth of her novels on Roman and post-Roman Britain, Rosemary Sutcliff is, as always, bang on the money: there is a great deal of heavy cold rain in this book. Her language is vigorous and frequently new-minted: we hear 'the faint tripple of a horse's hoofs' on the old Roman road; we see the moon striking 'little jinks of light' from a battered breastplate, while a busy stream goes 'brawling down the hill'; cornered, a snarling wild boar fixes us with 'eyes red like the sullen gleeds of a burnt-out fire'.

With such strong and urgent imagery, she conjures up the thorny, watery southern Kentish lands, perilous under wraiths of mist, over which the slippery moon floats 'like a curved feather . . . under the grey sweep of the tall marsh sky', where Owain is now enslaved. Across this treacherous landscape he goes in search of his master's lovely runaway mare Golden-eye, and helps to deliver her little foal, gleaming silver in the moonlight, whose destiny is to be the great white stallion of Thor. And nearby he plunges into a furious midnight sea to rescue the inert body of his master, his owner in fact, and take him home to his strong and stoical wife.

Like a brooding Sibelius symphony, the momentum of the book never lets up. It swirls and grows, from the echoing silence of the battlefield where Owain wakes, wounded, surrounded by the dead; via the desperate urgency of his panic, hunger and despair as he tries to survive on hares and hedgehogs, leaves and leverets; and it thunders right through the furious drama of the final pages to the sudden grandeur of the climax, when the dramatic arrival is announced of 'a tall proud man with cold eyes, and strong in his own esteem', coming ashore with a party of monks on the Isle of Thanet. It is Augustine, sent by Pope Gregory the Great to evangelize the marauding, heathen Anglo-Saxons, and to usher in nearly a thousand years of monasticism, with all its attendant advances in education, science and the arts.

There is a famous story that Gregory, after seeing some fair-haired boys being sold in the Roman slave market and being told they were Angles, remarked, '*Non Angli, sed angeli.*' Usually this is translated as 'Not Angles, but angels', though in *1066 and All That*, Sellar and Yeatman gloriously suggested another reading: they were not angels, said the Pope, but Anglicans. Sutcliff takes it one bathetic step further, having the powerful King Aethelbert of Kent, on hearing the witty epithet, stroke his beard and remark that along this coast they were, in actual point of fact, Jutes.

By now, though, young Owain has made a decision. After that last great battle against the invading Saxons many defeated Britons had made for Cornwall, hoping to buy space in a refugee boat taking them to a region of Gaul known as Armorica: they fled in such numbers that people joked they'd soon be calling it Brittany. But Owain had, perforce, stayed, living for ten years in occupied lands and working for the Saxon invaders. He is himself the descendant of an invader, of Aquila, hero of *The Eagle of the Ninth*, a Roman who first owned the great flawed emerald ring, carved with a dolphin, that gleams darkly through all the succeeding books and which now he proudly wears. His ancestors had settled, married and become integrated, as the Romano-British people. Now, Owain realizes that further assimilation is beginning. His Saxon masters, with their revered harpers and their exhausting sagas and riddles, are mostly good people, he has learned, no longer to be feared and hated. He will stay. Quite simply, like Schiller, he has realized the great truth that all men are brothers.

And an old, one-eyed prophet offers him another, lesser but nonetheless handy truth, learned in the course of a long life: 'There is nothing like the air that blows through apple trees for clearing a man's head from the fumes of overmuch mead.'

Rosemary Sutcliff's great – almost unique – skill is to weave seriously thrilling action, profound philosophy and even romance around the extant pillars of history, however few they are. She is trustworthy. To read her is to know, for sure, exactly what it was like to live in Sussex towards the end of the sixth century, and what it was to be a lad like Owain. This is such a great book, yet the flyleaf of my old paperback is stamped with the death sentence 'PULP COPY'. How excellent, then, that a beautiful new edition is now available, courtesy of Slightly Foxed, as part of a limited edition of her superb novels set in England during and after the Roman occupation.

SUE GAISFORD's journalism has appeared in many papers and magazines and still pops up here and there. An optimist, she is looking forward to the end of the current dark ages.

Slightly Foxed is reissuing all seven of Rosemary Sutcliff's Roman and post-Roman novels as a set in a limited and numbered cloth-bound edition of 2,000 copies.

The fifth title in the series, *Dawn Wind* (248pp), is now available (subscribers per copy for each title: UK & Eire £17, Overseas £19; non-subscribers: UK & Eire £18.50, Overseas £20.50). All prices include post and packing. Copies may be ordered by post (53 Hoxton Square, London N1 6PB), by phone (020 7033 0258) or via our website www.foxedquarterly.com.

The first four books in the series, *The Eagle of the Ninth*, *The Silver Branch*, *Frontier Wolf* and *The Lantern Bearers*, are still available. The final two books, *Sword Song* and *The Shield Ring*, will be published this coming September.

A Kind of Cosmic Refugee

NIGEL ANDREW

Julia Strachey was a writer of rare talent and originality who, in a lifetime of writing, managed to complete and publish only two novels and a number of sketches and short stories. I knew nothing of her until I happened to come across a Penguin reprint of those novels, *Cheerful Weather for the Wedding* and *An Integrated Man*. I was immediately bowled over by their brilliance and originality, and was surprised to discover that, in effect, they are all there is. What stopped this gifted writer from finishing and publishing more?

It's not that her work wasn't in demand. When *Cheerful Weather for the Wedding* was published in 1932, it met with a very warm reception. The literary editor of the *New Yorker* was so impressed that he wrote to Julia and offered to publish anything she cared to send him. Her response was to send nothing for a quarter of a century, until in 1958 she obliged with a sketch, which was duly published – but not until Julia had fought at length, and successfully, to have every single editorial alteration to her piece reversed. Clearly this was not a woman with a strong sense of how to build a literary career.

It isn't hard to see why *Cheerful Weather* so impressed its early readers. A cool, darkly comic account of an upper-middle-class wedding day in Dorset, it is brisk, deftly managed, sharply observed and

Julia Strachey, *Cheerful Weather for the Wedding* (1932)
Persephone · Pb · 136pp · £15 · ISBN 9781903155271
An Integrated Man (1951) and Frances Partridge's *Julia: A Portrait of Julia Strachey by Herself and Frances Partridge* (1983) are both out of print but we can obtain second-hand copies.

crisply written, without a word wasted. But, more than that, there is something in its tone that is unique – something 'airy and translucent', as one critic put it. Strachey herself said, rather cryptically, that her aim was to convey a 'phosphorescent' impression, and there is a strange luminosity about some of the descriptive passages, in which the author focuses her attention so fixedly on something that it seems to develop a faint unearthly glow. Here she is on a pot of ferns:

> The transparent ferns that stood massed in the window showed up very brightly, and looked fearful. They seemed to have come alive, so to speak. They looked to have just that moment reared up their long backs, arched their jagged and serrated bodies menacingly, twisted and knotted themselves tightly about each other, and darted out long forked and ribboning tongues from one to the other; and all as if under some terrible compulsion . . . they brought to mind travellers' descriptions of the jungles in the Congo – of the silent struggle and strangulation that vegetable life there consists in.

Strachey writes as if seeing those ferns for the first time, and her gaze is intense and appalled; she senses the menace lurking in the everyday objects that gather around us.

The dominant figure in *Cheerful Weather* is not the reluctant bride, who is quietly getting drunk – or her rejected suitor, who is rather more noisily getting drunk – but Mrs Thatcham, the bride's mother, a human whirlwind who is typically to be found

> rushing around the room on tiny feet, snapping off dead daffodil heads from the vases, pulling back window curtains, or pulling them forward, scratching on the carpet with the toe of her tiny shoe where a stain showed up. All this with a sharp anxiety on her face as usual – as though she had inadvertently swallowed a packet of live bumble-bees and was now beginning to feel them stirring about inside her.

Her constant refrain is 'I simply cannot understand it!', applied to anything that fails to conform to her view of how things should be.

There is another presence in the story, almost as strong as the human characters, and that is the brisk and blowy spring weather – the 'cheerful weather' (Mrs Thatcham's phrase) of the title. And weather – in this case the ever-changing weather of an English summer – is an equally strong presence in the second of Strachey's novels, *An Integrated Man*, first published (as *The Man on the Pier*) nearly twenty years later, in 1951. In this much longer work, events unfold over the length of a summer in the Thirties in a large country cottage, where a group of friends have gathered to talk, walk, eat and pass the time agreeably, while getting on with a little work. The 'integrated man' of the title is Ned Moon who, in the very first paragraph, declares that 'Everything in my life is well ordered and serene . . . My days are spent unharassed by pressures that torture and distort. At the age of forty-one, I'm bound to admit that I have become that fabulous beast, an "integrated man"!' If ever a man were riding for a fall, it is Ned Moon . . .

As in *Cheerful Weather*, Strachey's descriptive writing is highly distinctive, and summer in the country gives it plenty of scope:

> At ten minutes to one the postman had appeared . . . And certain cows, those that had lost their calves, on perceiving his red bicycle from afar, charged joyfully across the field in a bunch, imagining he was bringing back to them their stolen children. When they had realized their mistake, they had stood and trumpeted shrilly as usual for half an hour.
>
> Then luncheon – and a massed rendezvous of flies!
>
> . . . After lunch the cows had suddenly begun to bellow again. The flies, however, had dropped off to sleep.

And here, later, are the flies again:

All of a sudden the flies on the window-pane woke up and

started to rage together with a venomous zizzing. One amongst them began to boom deafeningly and to throw its scaly body repeatedly against the glass. Others, too, began to boom in the same echoing manner, and soon all of them together were hurling their scaly bodies against the pane. One could imagine that packets of tintacks were being showered again and again at the glass.

This highly strung, high-pitched style injects tension into what might otherwise seem placid and uneventful scenes (and *An Integrated Man* does get off to a slow start), but it comes fully into its own as Ned finally succumbs to the erotic fixation that is to prove his undoing. *An Integrated Man* is an extraordinarily frank and convincing account of the power of lust – and, in the end, the whole action turns on one sudden moment of recognition, conveyed in one startlingly raw paragraph. Impossible to say more without giving the plot away, but the climactic scene is an unforgettable piece of writing.

Both Julia Strachey's novels were in danger of being forgotten altogether when, very enterprisingly, Penguin reissued them in one volume in 1978, introducing them to a whole new readership. *Cheerful Weather* was also reissued by Persephone Books as recently as 2009. In between, in 1983, came an illuminating volume mixing autobiography and biography, *Julia: A Portrait of Julia Strachey by Herself and Frances Partridge*.

A friend of Julia's since childhood, Frances Partridge had inherited her dauntingly voluminous and chaotic papers, including her autobiographical writings. These fragments of memoir – which, typically, had never been organized into a finished book – are vivid and revealing, and include some of her best writing. Merging these with letters, diary entries and her own memories of Julia, Frances Partridge creates a compelling portrait of her friend, and one that goes a long way to explaining the peculiarities of her literary career.

A strikingly beautiful woman, Julia was also 'striking in her charm, her unhappiness and her formidable gifts'. And she was funny, spirited, exasperating and, despite everything, lovable. That striking unhappiness, though, is the key, and its roots lay deep. Her autobiographical writings begin with a rapturous, brightly coloured account of her childhood years in India, where her father Oliver (elder brother of Lytton Strachey) was a senior civil servant. Her mother, Ruby, was young, beautiful and affectionate, and Julia adored her. But this Indian paradise was lost with brutal abruptness when, at the age of 6, with no word of explanation, Julia was sent with her mother to Italy, then on, with only a nursemaid, to the gloomy London house

Julia Strachey, 1930s
© National Portrait Gallery, London

of a distant Strachey relation, where she was placed in the care of a fire-breathing elderly Scottish nanny. Both her parents had effectively washed their hands of her. This was the first, and hardest, betrayal of her life. She saw it as an expulsion from Paradise, and proof that there was something about her that meant that no one could truly love her.

This impression was confirmed when she was sent on from the London house to live in the country with the formidable Alys Pearsall Smith ('Aunt Loo', a family connection) and her brother, the then revered aphorist Logan, whose sparkling wit was shadowed by crushing (and, to a child, terrifying) depressions. This ménage, in which the two adult principals cordially loathed each other, is brilliantly, and often very comically, described by Julia. But then comes the terrible moment when Aunt Loo inadvertently, but shatteringly, confirms Julia's own opinion of her unlovableness. After this second betrayal, Julia sees herself as 'just a dismal, moth-eaten, seedy kind of freak', 'an alien – a kind of cosmic refugee, an unwanted changeling from another planet'.

Considering the emotional legacy of her childhood, it is a wonder that Julia managed to make as good a life for herself as she did, rackety, unsettled and ill-organized though it often was (two failed marriages, fatal attraction to much younger men, amphetamine addiction). To an extent, she was her own worst enemy, constantly inventing reasons for her failure to apply herself systematically to her craft, complaining of imaginary impediments, spending hours 'cogitating' (often lying in bed, with the covers drawn up to her nose) instead of actually writing. But to become a writer at all, she had to overcome not only her emotional problems but also a crippling dual legacy of Strachey perfectionism – the Stracheys had to be best at everything – and, from the Pearsall Smiths, intense self-criticism. We should be glad that, in all the circumstances, she managed to complete those two wonderful novels by which she will surely be remembered.

NIGEL ANDREW is a writer, reviewer and blogger. He has recently written *The Mother of Beauty* (2019), about the golden age of English church monuments and other matters of life and death.

Walking for the Sun and the Wind

CHRIS SAUNDERS

I think we can all agree on the restorative qualities of a country walk. Certainly, since I moved to Sussex, I have come to value walking as much more than a basic mode of transport, surrounded as I am by the tranquillity of fields, footpaths and woods. I only wish I could convince my daughter of the splendours on our doorstep.

In my search for something to inspire my beloved refusenik I landed upon a little book by Stephen Graham called *The Gentle Art of Tramping* (1926), which has recently been reprinted in a handsome little hardback edition by Bloomsbury. My eyes have been opened to a far more profound approach to perambulation than I ever expected. Tramping, in this case, is approximately a cross between rambling and hiking, more serious than the one and less intense than the other, with an emphasis on living off the land, sleeping outdoors and ignoring wristwatches.

It is written by a real master of the art. Stephen Graham (1884–1975) was an adventurer and journalist best known for his accounts of his treks on foot in Russia. Books such as *A Vagabond in the Caucasus* and *With the Russian Pilgrims to Jerusalem* told not only of his huge feats of pedestrianism but also his enduring sympathy for working people. When he enlisted in the Scots Guards during the Great War, he eschewed a commission in order to enter the ranks as a private. He wrote movingly of the life of the recruit in *A Private in the Guards*, a critique of the army's method of building a soldier by breaking the

Stephen Graham, *The Gentle Art of Tramping* (1926)
Bloomsbury · Hb · 208pp · £12.99 · ISBN 9781448217243

man. In *The Gentle Art of Tramping* he transfers his vagrant skills and subversive instincts to a more intimate British setting because, as he very wisely says, 'There are thrills unspeakable in Rutland, more perhaps than on the road to Khiva. Quality makes good tramping, not quantity.'

For Graham, tramping is meditative and even creative, giving the walker the mental freedom to express simple joys: 'We sing as we walk, we walk as we sing, and the kilometres fall behind.' He wasn't the first writer to associate walking with songs and poetry. Wordsworth thought that the rhythms of walking bred the rhythms of poetry, as did Edward Thomas after him. In *A Literary Pilgrim in England* Thomas also wrote of the prodigious hiker George Borrow that:

> He walked for the sun and the wind, for the joy and pride of his prowess in walking, and to get from one place to the other. Therefore his writing . . . is just English open country.

You could say the same of Graham, whose aim in this book is to encourage the urban dweller to reconnect with the country and so with themselves. It is an aim that is, as he acknowledges, at odds with the general flow of modern life:

> You will discern that going tramping is at first an act of rebellion; only afterwards do you get free from rebelliousness as Nature sweetens your mind. Town makes men contentious; the country smooths out their souls.

As someone who commutes most days from country to town and back again, I can only concur, and apologize for my occasional contentiousness.

This is a book that speaks to our current age very loudly, despite being nearly a hundred years old. Of course, a lot of the practical advice is old-fashioned and, in some cases, baffling. Graham seems to want to build an open fire and brew a pot of coffee every five miles or so, which sounds like a lot of labour for very little reward and requires clanking around the countryside with a dirty great kettle on your back. The burden of necessaries that one carries should also, he maintains, be supplemented by books, writing-paper, a pen, cutlery (but not a fork), a box for butter, shaving equipment, mosquito netting, an air pillow and a glove for taking the coffee pot off the fire. Still, who am I to argue with the don of tramping, especially when he seems so wise on deeper matters? Graham was no dilettante. This book's philosophy of freedom and solidarity was hard-won through his own experience.

These days we are always being told that people are on a 'journey' of self-discovery, reaching a goal or achieving an aspiration. *The Gentle Art of Tramping* goes beyond anything so narrowly linear. On Graham's journeys, the destination is unimportant, as is time or any kind of direction. He rejects all those industrious, Victorian ideas of filling unforgiving minutes with sixty seconds' worth of distance run: 'No, take care of the hours and the minutes can go hang. Take care of your life and your days will be all right.' He also advocates throwing away maps and plans, and he scorns roads. Instead he favours the 'zigzag' walk, in which you take the first left, then the first right, then the first left and so on until, presumably, you reach a dead end or an angry bull.

It is here that he introduces a delightful element of gentle anarchy. Tramping is, indeed, a rebellious act:

> You are going to be very ill-mannered and stray on to other people's property. Granted that fundamental impertinence you must be as nice as possible about it; graciously lift your hat to the proprietor when you see him.

There will be trespassing, and there will also be scrounging from obliging farmers' wives and a little light theft in the scrumping of apples. Not only does he disregard modern notions of time and progress, but also, in the politest way possible, the basic rules of capitalist society.

Graham's world has a very particular ethos that separates it from that of the 'professional hobo', which is apparently tacitly understood by everyone as long as you have the right combination of charm and discretion when asking for food and shelter: 'You enter as a gentleman . . . In return for hospitality of the body . . . one should always give hospitality of the mind or spirit, sympathy, fellow-feeling, *bonhomie* . . .' Also, you should never take the last marrow.

The parallel tramping universe is irresistibly seductive. *The Gentle Art* is full of practical advice on boots and the need to avoid wet tweeds, but that is not really the point of the book. It is about defying the traps that the post-industrial world lays for us. It is a treatise against all of those qualities that built the Empire, the same qualities he saw in the army – ambition, industriousness and competition. Anyone entering the tramping world with those values has got it all wrong:

> I listen with pained reluctance to those who claim to have walked forty or fifty miles a day. But it is a pleasure to meet the man who has learned the art of going slowly, the man who disdained not to linger in the happy morning hours, to watch, to exist. Life is like a road; you hurry, and the end of it is grave.

In a funny way, he wants readers to regain their sense of themselves and their country by forgetting all those characteristics that we are told make us British in the first place. It is such an attractive proposition precisely because it is so contrary to our conditioning and so lyrically expressed.

Graham is well aware that the escape to the country is for almost all of his readers temporary, restricted to weekends and holidays. He is realistic enough to acknowledge that people can't live their whole lives in his parallel world. The economics of modern life, alas, just don't allow it. Rather, he sees it as a way to preserve sanity and perspective, and as a great social leveller: 'It is no small part of the gentle art of tramping to accept the simple and humble role and not to crave respect, honour, obeisance.' A staunch democrat, he would no doubt point out that, once you have paid for your coffee pot, sturdy boots and pocket edition of Horace, tramping is, unlike most modern therapies, open to all and absolutely free.

Still, I haven't been able to tempt my daughter out for a long tramp. An ardent sportswoman, she considers an activity without goals or competition to be pointless, even though that very pointlessness is, in fact, the point. Also, I have to recognize that five days sleeping on rocks and living on wild plums isn't for everyone. But I think that as long as you abide by Graham's most fundamental piece of advice you will be alright: 'one should avoid lying down in a basket of snakes'.

CHRIS SAUNDERS is the managing director of Henry Sotheran Ltd, Britain's oldest antiquarian bookseller. He is also a writer on bookish matters and runs the literary blog *Speaks Volumes*. He shares his house in East Sussex with his wife, daughter and hundreds of books, some of which he's read.

Bruised, Shocked, but Elated

SELINA HASTINGS

I first met Sybille Bedford in London in the early 1980s when an old friend of mine, Patrick Woodcock, who at the time was Sybille's doctor, invited us both to dinner. As a keen admirer of Sybille's writing, I was thrilled at the prospect.

I was the first to arrive, a little nervous and full of anticipation. Soon afterwards Sybille made her entrance, a small, neat figure with short grey hair, dressed in trousers and waistcoat, a red-and-white spotted kerchief tucked into the neck of her shirt. Patrick introduced us, Sybille nodded acknowledgement, and from that moment on she completely ignored me, addressing all her conversation to Patrick. The chief topic, I remember, was her current infatuation with a woman artist in Richmond, only interrupted by a detailed analysis of the food – Patrick was an excellent cook – and of the wine we were drinking, both always a matter of supreme importance to Sybille.

I returned home feeling slightly snubbed, and it was several years before I encountered her again. This time it was at dinner in the flat of another old friend, Stanley Olson, a great gourmet and wine connoisseur. That occasion was very different: Sybille was charming, talkative and highly amusing, and from then on I saw her at fairly regular intervals, every few months or so. We met at her tiny flat in Chelsea, or at my house or in restaurants, and once she asked me to an oenophiles' gathering to pay homage to a rare claret, which of course was way above my station. We also talked on the telephone,

Sybille Bedford, *A Visit to Don Otavio* (1953)
Eland · Pb · 320pp · £12.99 · ISBN 9780907871873

long conversations which usually started with Sybille complaining about some domestic irritation – a plumber who had failed to turn up, noisy neighbours on the floor above – but which almost always evolved into some fascinating recollection of her extraordinary, and often harrowing, past.

In 2002 I completed a life of the novelist Rosamond Lehmann, who had been a good friend to Sybille. Sybille sent me a complimentary letter, and, although I didn't know it at the time, it was that book that made her decide she wanted me as her biographer. This I learned only after her death. Although I knew something of her life and was excited by the prospect of writing about her, it was not until I had spent several months reading her papers at the Ransom Center in Texas that I realized just how rich and extraordinary her story is.

*

Born in Germany in 1911, Sybille, after her father's death, had moved to France at the age of 15 to live with her mother. And it was France that remained her base until 1940, when she was forced to flee, her identity as both German and Jewish a sudden and serious threat to her safety. Arrived in America, she spent the war years in New York, increasingly anxious, once hostilities had ceased, to return to Europe. But from the moment peace was declared a vast exodus began, the waiting lists for transatlantic passage seemingly endless, the price of tickets far above what Sybille could afford. Eventually, realizing she had little hope of leaving the continent, she decided instead to go south, to travel to another country, eager to investigate a different history and culture.

Throughout most of her long life, Sybille remained a keen traveller, almost constantly on the move, living in England, France, Italy, in her middle age writing many articles about her extensive journeys through Europe. Prone to anxiety, she never liked to travel alone, and was nearly always accompanied by one of a series of lovers with whom she lived over the years. While in New York Sybille had begun an affair with a woman almost fifteen years her senior, Esther Murphy, sister of Gerald Murphy, the close friend of Scott Fitzgerald. Tall, un-gainly, very masculine in appearance, Esther was kind-hearted, clever and formidably well-read, given to talking for hours on end, drink and cigarette always to hand. With the war over, the two women spent hours poring over maps, examining the possibilities of South America, of Peru, Uruguay, Montevideo, all of which turned out to be far too expensive. So they settled on Mexico.

In the event, Sybille and Esther were to spend eight months in the country, a period vividly recalled in *A Visit to Don Otavio*. Passionately curious, Sybille was an avid explor-er, keen to discover as much as she could, while Esther, referred to as 'E' in the book, remained the 'born anti-traveller'. 'God, she hated to travel,' Sybille recalled. 'I laugh when I think of her in Mexico . . . this tall Don Quixote figure, with a head like Jefferson, bowing to everybody and saying, "Viva Mexico," with an American accent. It's the only Span-ish she learned.'

Arriving in Mexico City after a long, frequently delayed journey by train, the two women settled into a hotel, after which Sybille imme-diately set off on her own to explore the city. Although bewildered by the noisy, crowded streets, she instantly became fascinated by the sheer foreignness of her surroundings.

As one picks one's way over mangoes and avocado pears one is tumbled into the gutter by a water-carrier, avoids a Buick saloon and a basin of live charcoal, skips up again scaring a

76

tethered chicken, shies from an exposed deformity and bumps into a Red Indian gentleman in a tight black suit.

Over the next few days, Sybille, accompanied by a benignly indifferent Esther, visited many of the sights of the capital, churches and palaces, galleries and museums, as well as the murals of Diego Rivera in the Palacio Nacional.

During the initial weeks in Mexico City one of the great pleasures for Sybille was to sample the local cuisine. From her childhood in Germany, and under the influence of her gourmet father, she had grown passionately interested in food and wine. And now, after years of the bland, boring fare of America, she could hardly wait to sample Mexican cooking. Seated in a local restaurant soon after arrival, she assesses with great concentration every mouthful of the long succession of courses. First two kinds of soup, then omelettes, after which came

> two spiny fishes covered in tomato sauce . . . Two thin beef-steaks like the soles of children's shoes . . . two platefuls of bird bones, lean drumstick and pointed wing smeared with some brown substance . . . We eat heartily of everything. Everything tastes good, nearly everything is good.

Rather less palatable is the wine. 'I sniff before tasting, so the shock when it comes is not as devastating as it might have been . . . Cheap ink dosed with prune juice and industrial alcohol, as harsh on the tongue as a carrot-grater.'

Over the following weeks and months the two women were constantly on the move, travelling to Cuernavaca and Morelia, to Mazatlán, Acapulco and Veracruz. Together they covered hundreds of miles, cooped up on rackety trains that were always late, in taxis driven at hair-raising speed, on crowded buses stuffed to the rooftop with turkeys and pigs. Yet despite the discomfort Sybille was enthralled, while Esther remained calmly detached, rarely looking up from her volume of Trollope or Jane Austen. 'I am more and more enchanted with Mexico,' Sybille reported to a friend, 'but Esther does not like to move, and stalks past colonial palaces and Aztec pyramids much as Doctor Johnson must have stalked through the Hebrides.'

Throughout their journey, all is observed with close attention, Sybille graphically describing her surroundings, vigorously engaging with the characters encountered en route – nuns, hoteliers, shopkeepers, as well as resident expatriates from Europe and America, many of the last regarded with a frigid distaste. As they continue with their rackety road trip, Sybille and Esther experience varying degrees of comfort. Arriving in Guadalajara at a magnificent sixteenth-century palace, now a hotel, they discover the staircase to their first-floor room has yet to be installed and there is no running water. ('"There doesn't seem to be any water in our bathroom." "Of course not, Señora. It has not been laid on. One thing after another. Perhaps next year?"') Elsewhere, by contrast, they find themselves living in luxury in exquisitely serene surroundings, on an estate on the shores of Lake Chapala belonging to an eccentric nobleman, 'Don Otavio'.

In the book the property is depicted as a private house, although in fact it was a hotel, the Villa Monte Carlo, its owner Don Guillermo Brizuela, who, like his fictional counterpart, Don Otavio, was generous, courteous, charming and effeminate. 'He was wearing white flannels . . . [and a] shirt decorated with sea-horses. A bunch of gold holy medals tinkled in the open neck . . . He turned out one of the kindest men I ever met.' Over the weeks spent staying with Don Guillermo, Sybille came to know a number of his friends, family and neighbours, they and their social interconnections providing rich material for the partly fictionalized account which she was eventually to produce. So enchanted were the two women by the hotel and its owner that they decided to stay on for some time, and it was here, 'one warm night, on the terrace of a hacienda, lying on a deckchair under the sub-tropical sky', that the idea came to Sybille of writing about her Mexican experience.

In the event it would be over two years before she began work on the book, by which time she had returned to Europe and was living in Rome. *A Visit to Don Otavio*, originally entitled *The Sudden View*, was the first of Sybille's books to be published. Although from her earliest days she had been determined to write, her previous attempts had been unsuccessful: three works of fiction completed during the 1930s had been turned down. Now, however, she had found her voice. *Don Otavio* is a superb accomplishment, an intensely involving traveller's tale that reads like a novel. ('Of course it's a novel,' admitted the author some years later. 'I didn't take a single note while I was in Mexico.') The book appeared first in Britain in 1953, a year later in the United States; widely praised, and subsequently translated into Italian, French and German, it has hardly been out of print since.

Encouraged by such acclaim, Sybille immediately began work on a new project. A novel, entitled *A Legacy*, it was to prove a remarkable success and to establish her permanently as a distinguished member of the profession of which from her earliest days she had aspired to be part.

SELINA HASTINGS has written biographies of Nancy Mitford, Evelyn Waugh, Rosamond Lehmann, Somerset Maugham, of her father, *The Red Earl*, and Sybille Bedford.

The Great Self-Examiner

ANTHONY WELLS

Can anyone reconcile us with death?

Michel de Montaigne, one of the great sages of the Renaissance, tried his best; and he was trying to reconcile himself as much as any readers he might have. 'We must always be booted and ready to go,' he writes in an early essay. To be ready we need to familiarize ourselves with this final destination. 'So,' he tells us, 'I have formed the habit of having death continually present, not merely in my imagination, but in my mouth . . . He who would teach men to die would teach them to live.'

When in 1571 Montaigne retired from his position at the parliament of Bordeaux to the estate he had recently inherited, he wasn't yet 40. Though no subject preoccupied him so much as death, he was still in good health, still free of the crippling kidney stones that would make his later years a torment. But to his surprise, all set as he was to dedicate the rest of his days to 'liberty, tranquillity and leisure', he found himself overwhelmed by depression. The only remedy he could think of was to write, as he explains to a friend in one essay:

It was a melancholy humour, and consequently a humour very

Montaigne's *Essays* were translated into English by Florio in 1603. Several other translations have followed, among them those by Donald Frame (1943) and M. A. Screech (1991). I have quoted from all three. Florio's perhaps best conveys Montaigne's idiosyncratic style; Frame's is fluent and easier to read, and helpfully gives all of Montaigne's quotations from Greek and Latin in English; Screech, the most scholarly, provides a wealth of background information and also makes sure he translates a spade as a spade.

hostile to my natural disposition, produced by the gloom of the solitude into which I had cast myself some years ago, that first put into my head this daydream of meddling with writing.

He could think of nothing to write about, however; so, with no other subject suggesting itself, 'I offered myself to myself as theme and subject matter.' If others could make portraits of themselves in pictures, why shouldn't he portray himself with the pen?

In doing so, Montaigne takes as his watchword a motto from Plato: 'Do what thou hast to do, and know thyself.' To which he adds a characteristic rider: 'Whoever would do what he has to do would see that the first thing he must learn is to know what he is.' It was to learn what he was, and in the process learn what humankind was, that this first writer of essays (in French, literally, tests or attempts) embarked on his work.

What does he find when he examines this thing, his own self, critically and dispassionately? Something very shaky, very susceptible to outside influences – the weather, for one – variable, inconsistent, self-contradictory. 'Others fashion man, I repeat him; and represent a particular one, but ill made, and whom, were I to form anew, he should be far other than he is; but he is now made.'

Other people may believe they are wise and reasonable, in control of their destinies; all he can say is that he can lay claim to very little of that. Not only is he not master of his own body; his mind is also out of control. When he first withdrew to the privacy of the tower-cum-library on his Périgord estate, he thought the best he could do was to leave his mind in total idleness, calmly thinking of itself. What did he find? That 'it bolted off like a runaway horse', giving birth to so many chimeras and fantastic monstrosities that he began to keep a record of them, 'hoping in time to make [his] mind ashamed of itself'.

It is not only the weather, events and our bodies that play havoc with our plans and intentions; emotions do likewise. Crucially, they unbalance our judgement: anger, for instance, to which he devotes a whole essay, or fear, and its child, cowardice. From cowardice springs the cruelty which Montaigne despised, not least because he witnessed so much of it in the religious wars that raged with such ferocity in his own area of France: 'What is it that makes all our quarrels end in death nowadays?' he asks. 'Whereas our fathers knew degrees of vengeance we now begin at the end and straightway talk of nothing but killing. What causes that, if not cowardice?'

Montaigne hates excess of all kinds. We human beings are so inconsistent, so changeable, that we should learn to live within our limitations. Similarly with opinions: they vary from one person to another but even within one person they can be self-contradictory and change from one day to the next. By piling up examples and counter-examples, and arguing first this way then that, Montaigne thinks aloud to himself, trying to sift the true from the false, and work out what is useful for him, and us, in living our lives.

Having discovered himself to be comprised of so many 'feeble and failing pieces', he is struck by the 'over-high opinion which Man has of himself'. Humankind in general, whether ancient or modern, has few grounds for believing itself the crown of creation. Are we really so superior to the animals, he asks. Why do we assume that the animals are just dumb brutes obeying only their instincts? 'When I play with my cat,' Montaigne wonders, 'how do I know that she is not passing time with me rather than I with her?' As for the supposed superiority of European civilization, the Spanish conquistadors' treatment of the peoples of the New World (of which Montaigne sought out first-hand accounts) was clear evidence of how little claim to moral superiority the Europeans of his time had over other peoples.

Montaigne was avid for information about other peoples; he loved travelling partly for that reason, noting with relish the differences in manners and the variety of customs and behaviour. 'I am of the opinion that no fantasy so mad can fall into human imagination that meets not with the example of some public custom,' he writes, going on to list a number of odd customs, including people 'who, when the King spitteth, the most favoured Lady in his court stretcheth forth her hand; and in another country, where the noblest about him stoop to the ground to gather his ordure in some fine linen cloth'.

Clothes were another example of this variety, as were eating habits, religious rites and relations between the sexes. As far as he could tell, from his reading and from talking to people, these varied across the world, from the New World to China. They were all evidence of the power of custom, which makes up so great a part of what we consider our nature. 'We call contrary to nature what happens contrary to custom.' Nature, Montaigne argues, following one of his favourite schools of philosophy, the Stoics, embodies Reason: our duty as human beings is to live in conformity with her laws, which are universal, and then with the customs of our particular place and time.

And the first of Nature's laws is to live virtuously. However, virtue for Montaigne is not rejection of the pleasures of life; on the contrary, the good life consists in knowing how to enjoy those pleasures. The key is to resist the temptation to extremes of enjoyment, or of any behaviour: it is no better to shun pleasures entirely than to pursue them to excess. In fact, forgoing them completely is, he thinks, easier than enjoying them reasonably. One such pleasure is drinking, which he says we should make 'more expansive and vigorous' in our daily habits, especially as we get older, since drinking 'is almost the last pleasure that the years steal from us'. Try telling that to our modern health czars!

Even on the subject of virtue Montaigne is never didactic, 'feeling myself too ill-instructed to instruct others'. Nor should one look too much to scholars or books for instruction, he advises: from books he seeks only to give himself pleasure 'by honest amusement' or to encounter the learning that 'instructs me in how to die well and live well'. As for scholars, 'I have seen in my time hundreds of craftsmen and ploughmen wiser and happier than University Rectors – and whom I would rather be like'. Acutely aware of his own (and our) faults and failings, Montaigne wants rules of life which are fitting for such an imperfect creature. His attempt to understand himself has revealed so many inconsistencies, inadequacies and contradictions in his make-up that neither he nor anyone else has grounds for pontificating. This is why he has put his thoughts down in the form of essays – they are still tentative: 'If my mind could gain a firm footing, I would not make essays, I would make decisions; but it is always in apprenticeship and on trial.'

His difficulty in reaching a view was one reason why Montaigne loved conversation. He could not stand people who were over-enamoured of their own views or so arrogant as to dismiss others' arguments out of hand, a vice he thought lay at the root of the cruelty of the religious wars. 'What a loathsome malady it is', he writes, 'to believe you are so right that you convince yourself that nobody can think the opposite.' People needed to take time to think, weigh up all the arguments and learn to exercise their judgement. Judgement is for Montaigne the critical human faculty, since by exercising it we have the chance to live the moderate, tranquil life we should seek.

Montaigne's style of writing is in keeping with his conversational approach. He does not aim to write beautifully: his purpose is to try to describe what he is and to pin down his thoughts. All sorts of stories and illustrations, tales and sayings are grist to his mill, many taken from the Greeks and Romans – Montaigne's first language in childhood was Latin – or the Bible. He also takes examples from his own times, though less readily – he was aware of the potential dangers of talking freely about contemporary matters in a time of civil war.

The longer Montaigne spent on his essays, the keener he became to throw off the shackles of convention when it came to talking about our human lives, particularly our physical lives. One of his insistent themes is how closely knitted together are our bodies and our souls. We are physical beings and must not spurn or deride the body and its pleasures: 'For it is indeed reasonable . . . that the body should not follow its appetites to the disadvantage of the mind; but why is it not also reasonable that the mind should not pursue its appetites to the disadvantage of the body?'

His wish to be sincere required straightforwardness of language. Erudite works treated their subjects in too artificial a style, he thought. In contrast, he tells us, 'I have ordered myself to dare to say all that I dare to do.' One area to which he applied this principle was sex.

Well now, leaving books aside and talking more simply and plainly, I find that sexual love is nothing but the thirst for enjoyment of that pleasure within the object of our desire, and that Venus is nothing but the pleasure of unloading our balls.

This in the case of men, clearly, but he does not believe women are so different in their motivation. Males and females are cast in the same mould: 'except for education and custom,' he argues, 'the difference is not great'. Like any other pleasure, though, sex 'becomes vitiated by a lack of either moderation or discretion'. The key, as in so many other aspects of life, is to follow 'the fine and level road that Nature has traced for us'.

As he reached the end of his great undertaking – by the time of the second edition of the *Essays* (1588), he had written 107 of them, ranging in length from a single page to 170 pages – he laid increasing stress on the virtues of experience over intellectual knowledge. In his last essay, he gives us his conclusion: 'Nothing is so beautiful, so right, as acting as a man should: nor is any learning so arduous as knowing how to live this life naturally and well.'

As for death, the subject to which he has returned so frequently, by his last essays his thinking has changed. 'If you don't know how to die, don't worry,' he comforts us. 'Nature will tell you what to do on the spot, fully and adequately.' You will only have to follow the example of his own farm workers at the time of a recent plague: 'Here a man, healthy, was already digging his grave; others lay down in them while still alive. And one of my labourers, with his hands and feet, pulled the earth over him as he was dying. Was that not taking shelter so as to go to sleep more comfortably?'

Montaigne himself died in 1592. In the twenty years of his 'retirement' – interrupted by a return to Bordeaux in the 1580s for two spells as its mayor – he had simultaneously invented a new literary form and written a book of such winning, entertaining and thought-provoking candour and originality that it would be read for centuries. One early reader of Montaigne is thought to have been William Shakespeare. What greater inspiration could there be to read the *Essays* for yourself?

Like Montaigne, ANTHONY WELLS has retired from the world of work and has plans to write a book. There any comparison ends.

Making a Meal of It

YSENDA MAXTONE GRAHAM

Plot: towards lunchtime, a male employee in a large corporate office building (the first-person narrator) discovers that the shoelace of his left shoe has snapped precisely twenty-eight hours after the right one snapped: a thought-provoking coincidence. Clutching his Penguin copy of Marcus Aurelius' *Meditations* and pausing first for a pee in the men's room, he descends the escalator to buy a bag of popcorn, a hot-dog, a cookie, a carton of milk and a new pair of shoelaces. Then he goes back up the escalator to his office, carrying his small bags. That's it.

Yet a mass of human delight and anxiety, and indeed the very essence of the workings of the human mind, are distilled in Nicholson Baker's *sui generis* 144-page chronicle of a single American office lunch-hour, a novel in which no tiny, mundane, daily habitual action is considered too small to examine and meditate on at length.

Baker's ultra-minimalist *The Mezzanine* made a great impression on me when it first came out in 1988, the time when hot-air hand-dryers were starting to replace hand-towel dispensers. And the particular sentence in it that has stayed with me ever since is this: 'Come to your senses, World!' – the capital 'W' denoting that the narrator was referring not to the world, but to World Corporation Dryers. His detailed rant, unleashed by reading the text on the World Dryer – 'this quick sanitary method dries hands more thoroughly, prevents chapping – and keeps washrooms free of towel waste' – goes on for a

Nicholson Baker, *The Mezzanine* (1988)
Granta · Pb · 144pp · £10 · ISBN 9781783786381

page and a half. What if you need to dry your face, he fumes? 'Out of desperation, real and true desperation that I have experienced, you resort to the toilet paper.' But 'as soon as you dampen it with warm water, it wilts to a semi-transparent pûrée in your fingers'. Spot on.

Also, for the last thirty-two years I've thought about *The Mezzanine* every time I've stood on an escalator. In his musings on the workings of daily life, Baker drew from the subconscious to the conscious our awareness that escalator bannister rails move at a very slightly different pace from escalator stairs, so one's elbow becomes more (or less) bent by the end of the ride. The narrator works out that, in his office escalator's case, 'the handrail was lapped every fifty revolutions'.

Reading the novel again this week, in the age of the Dyson Air Blade, I was just as charmed, although much of the office paraphernalia (stapled memos, cigarette vending-machines, rubber date stampers) has now disappeared. There's more nostalgia today in some of the book's pleasures. For example, the exquisitely accurate description of the workings of a Tetra Pak milk carton (called a Sealtest carton in the USA) made me miss those cartons. The narrator marvels at

> the radiant idea that you tore apart one of the triangular eaves of the carton, pushing its wing flap back, using the stiffness of its own glued seam against itself, forcing the seal inside out, without ever having to touch it, into a diamond-shaped opening which became a real pourer, a better pourer than a circular bottle opening or a pitcher's mouth because you could create a very fine stream of milk . . .

The carton inventor's genius fills him with 'jealousy and satisfaction'. But, he adds, 'it took my mother a few years before she stopped absent-mindedly trying to tear open the wrong side of the carton, despite my having lectured her on the fact that one triangle was much more heavily glued than the other'.

Yes! One's mother (or aunt or grandmother) did do exactly that, for 'years', in those bewildering post-milk-bottle days; and even we ourselves occasionally tried to open it at the wrong end. It's delicious to read about these daily mechanical actions, described by this writer who combines a boyish, sciencey fascination for How Things Work with a poet's ability to express and delight in it.

As well as marvelling at how things work, Baker can be deeply pained by flawed inventions, such as the new plastic straw.

> I stared in disbelief the first time a straw rose up from my can of soda and hung out over the table, barely arrested by burrs in the underside of the metal opening . . .
>
> How could the straw engineers have made so elementary a mistake, designing a straw that weighed less than the sugar water in which it was intended to stand?

For such a short book, *The Mezzanine* is actually a very slow read. This is because of the footnotes. A tiny '1' above a word such as 'straw' or 'doorknob' forces you to dart your eyes downwards in mid-sentence to a long (but definitely necessary, you feel, if this book is going to do full justice to a man's actual thoughts in his lunch-hour) digression on straws or doorknobs, in a much smaller font. The doorknob footnote mentions how the narrator's father used to hang his ties over the glass-faceted doorknob at home, and how 'once in a while a tie would ripple to the floor, having been gradually cranked into disequilibrium by many turnings'. I think our minds do go off on these long footnotey tangents in the mid-sentence of our thoughts. This tangent model seems a more accurate depiction of how the mind works than the Joycean stream-of-consciousness model. We disappear down the rabbit holes of our own mental digressions.

Sometimes the footnotes go on for three-quarters of a page, or more; the longest one, about gramophone styluses, goes on for four pages of eye-achingly tiny text, with only four lines of 'real' text at the top of each page, so they look like pages from the Arden *Hamlet*. When you've finished reading this vast digression (not one of my favourites, as the details didn't resonate with me, and not all of them do), you then have to flick back to the tiny 'I' in the middle of a now long-forgotten sentence – reminding me of flicking back to a da capo in Bach.

Baker is good on the atmosphere and daily realities of office life. He's close to the bone when he mentions the 'efficient little sniffs' his colleagues make when they walk past his desk 'to signal to us and to themselves that they are busy and walking somewhere for a very good reason'. I definitely make those 'efficient little sniffs' in my house, when virtuously lugging the washing basket past rooms in which other members of the family are sitting.

His appreciation of the man whose job it is to polish the escalator rails has an Edward Hopper-ish charm. The cleaner simply stands at the bottom of the moving bannister, holding his cloth against it. 'This guy probably knew every landmark of that rubber handrail', including 'the fusion scar where the two ends had been spliced together to close the loop'. (I'll look for that 'scar' the next time I'm on an escalator.) The narrator takes care, when he steps on, to grasp the handrail the man hasn't been polishing. 'It would have been odd to grasp the handrail he had been polishing – like walking on a newly mopped floor: it would have heightened the always nearby sense of futility of building maintenance.' This novel is awash with small but important human truths like that.

Sitting on a bench (at last) after the 28-page pre-lunch men's-room session which covers everything from contagious bathroom tune-whistling to his difficulty in peeing in a communal space, the narrator admits he's not even enjoying the Marcus Aurelius. He purchased the book because he'd happened to like the sample sentence on p.168 that he'd read in the shop. But he had liked it 'better than anything I came across in later consecutive reading'. How often have we done that – bought a book on the strength of a sample sentence read in a bookshop, which turns out to be the only good sentence? Often. The problem with reading, he remarks, is that 'you always had to pick up again at the very thing that had made you stop the day before'. Good point – and the same with knitting, I find.

Very bizarrely, the narrator informs us that this lunch-hour, the one in which his second shoelace broke, in fact happened to him years ago, when he was 23, and he's now in his mid-thirties. What's that all about? It might be pure wit on Baker's part: building up our hopes that something important is going to happen in this lunch-hour singled out for recollection, only to leave us with the bathos of the main event being the broken shoelace. But perhaps Baker is also showing us that every random hour of our lives deserves to be put under the microscope and be paid full homage.

One of the longest footnotes, towards the end of the book, is actually about footnotes. The narrator explains why he likes them – but only if they're written by the author, and not by some scholar who tediously footnotes and explains every single tricky word of a poem. 'Digression is sometimes the only way to be thorough,' he surmises; and footnotes 'offer reassurances that the pursuit of truth doesn't have clear outer boundaries'. They are 'the finer-suckered surfaces that allow tentacular paragraphs to hold fast to the wider reality of the library'.

His tangents are not always the same as mine; I haven't spent years of my life meditating on the workings of escalators or shoelaces; but in revealing his own private mental digressions Baker's narrator encourages us to admit to our own. We might all have similar habits of thought, but the minute details of what we think about reveal us all to be very different from each other, and alone.

YSENDA MAXTONE GRAHAM is the author of three Slightly Foxed Editions: *Mr Tibbits's Catholic School*, *The Real Mrs Miniver* and *Terms & Conditions*. Her latest book, *British Summer Time Begins: The School Summer Holidays, 1930–1980*, was published in 2020.

Shelving My Assumptions

URSULA BUCHAN

Last year, in response to a public consultation on the viability of my local public library, I offered to volunteer my unskilled services every Friday afternoon. This was my small way of signalling to the county council how precious a resource I believed the library to be, even if I hadn't visited it that often since my children left school. (I would need three lifetimes to read the books already residing on my own shelves.) The library is situated in a reasonably, but not excessively, prosperous small town, with a mixed-age population; like a thousand others across the country, I guess. I was gratefully welcomed by the professional librarians and set to work putting returned books back in their proper place on the shelves.

In my working life, I have met professional archivists, since I sometimes carry out research in correspondence and newspaper collections. They are courteous but firm, and sticklers for the rules, since they are in charge of irreplaceable, and often very valuable, historical documents. Librarians in public libraries are altogether more relaxed. If my experience is anything to go by, they are endlessly patient with stupid questions, surprisingly tolerant of noise, and extremely good with children. My shelving activities free them to do what they do best, which is to think up imaginative craft-based schemes to catch the interest of readers, especially youthful ones.

The most challenging stacking task, I soon discovered, concerns children's books. The minute differences between the various publishers' reading schemes make me frantic, and the lurid covers of young fiction give me a headache. (It must be worse for children, who have so much sharper eyesight than me.) I easily tire of shelving books featuring charmless dinosaurs or winsome aliens. I was also initially surprised to discover that many children's books are written by people who have made their reputations in strikingly different spheres. I had been under the impression that children's fiction was a specialized skill, but obviously not if any old Nobel-winning physicist, Premier League footballer or prima ballerina can get published.

In my role as amateur bookshelver, I have discovered that I am both a Dewey fetishist and an alphabet obsessive, aspiring conscientiously to reassign the books that careless readers put back in the wrong place. It has made me weirdly intolerant of variant spellings of names. Why can't all 'Mc's' be 'Mac's' or vice versa? And don't get me started on the names of Scandi noir writers.

My experiences in this library have also taught me how little I knew about the reading habits of the nation. I now realize that for half a lifetime I have been wasting precious energy writing high-minded, exhaustively researched, carefully edited, annotated and illustrated non-fiction, which frankly leaves my fellow citizens almost completely cold.

The starkest jolt I received occurred as soon as I was shown round the library on my first day. I discovered that the section devoted to crime fiction vastly outstripped in size those of history, biography, literary fiction, crafts, gardening, cooking, travel and even romantic fiction. And I now understand why. It is not uncommon on a Friday afternoon to see a dozen elderly ladies decant from their shopping bags a pile of paperbacks with strident, garish covers featuring bloody knives, hangmen's nooses or spooky alleyways; these, I'm guessing (since I have not the nerve to read them myself), enfold tales of murder, mayhem, corruption, cruelty and every variety of bodily fluid. These old ladies may be frail of frame but they are strong of stomach. Only a little research online convinced me that a number of authors of whom I had never until that moment heard – James Patterson, Jo Nesbo, David Baldacci, Peter James, for example – had made tidy sums and glowing reputations by writing lengthy series of gory thrillers.

That was by no means the only surprise, however. I also had no idea until I seriously studied the shelves that there were in the world so many 'romances' which feature (and I only slightly exaggerate) a doughty, sparky, sassy divorcée, running away from her past by opening a teashop in an attractive village. Her success and chance of future happiness are in the balance,

Daniel Macklin

for there is a strong risk that she will be thwarted by the machinations of a glowering landlord, with a chiselled profile and a tragic past. These volumes have bright, appealing primary colour covers and simple blurbs, on which the word 'bestseller' appears prominently. Should these books be written by Americans, the words '*New York Times* bestseller' seem well-nigh obligatory.

Although, as an untrained volunteer, I can never aspire to access to the library's computer, I have sufficiently insinuated myself with the kindly librarians for them to be willing to let me loose with the 'dead stock list' – especially if they are preoccupied with creating the next Star Wars or Harry Potter children's event for the following morning. The 'dead stock list' consists of titles that have not been borrowed by any reader for at least a year, and thus can be happily consigned to the 'for sale' pile, since the library is always chronically short of shelf space, especially to accommodate the aforementioned gory thrillers. However, it is very rare for a crime novel to find its way on to this list; it is in the far reaches of biography, history and foreign languages that the axe is inclined to fall. Most vulnerable of all are the books in the small 'Classics' section. The first time I was given the list, I was alarmed to see *The Pilgrim's Progress* on it. With a look of wild surmise, I took the greatest Christian allegory ever written in

English to the librarian's desk, only to be reassured that she wouldn't dream of letting John Bunyan go. All I needed to do, she advised, was to swipe my library card at the machine, take the book out and then immediately return it, so that it appeared on the computer as having been borrowed. Thus did *Adam Bede*, *A Room with a View* and *Eugénie Grandet* survive the cull. I make a habit nowadays of taking a few 'Classics' out each Friday, just as an insurance policy. I have even been known to take them home to read.

Despite the obvious rewards, URSULA BUCHAN has decided not to take up crime writing, but to remain working in the less dangerous sphere of non-fiction. Her biography of John Buchan, *Beyond the Thirty-Nine Steps*, was published in 2019.

The *Slightly Foxed* Crossword No. 12: Answers

Across: 1 ANCIENTS 5 GRIMES 10 PORTERHOUSE BLUE 11 RISINGS 12 HEELING 13 AMERICAN 15 TAWSE 18 AESOP 20 ADNATION 23 POLLITT 25 STRYVER 26 GOODBYE TO BERLIN 27 NEARER 28 WEBSTER'S

Down: 1 ASPERN 2 CHRISTMAS 3 ELEANOR 4 TAHRS 6 RE-ELECT 7 MALFI 8 SPENGLER 9 BUCHANAN 14 CRABTREE 16 WOODVILLE 17 HARPAGON 19 PLIABLE 21 TURNERS 22 DRONES 24 LEONA 25 SLOPE

Bibliography

Coming attractions

SUE GAISFORD gets a fresh angle on Chaucer · CHARLES ELLIOTT admires some literary sleuths · FRANCES DONNELLY takes a break on a lake · PATRICK WELLAND follows the fortunes of a Jewish family · LESLEY DOWNER learns a new language · MICHAEL BARBER enjoys an undiplomatic diary · POSY FALLOWFIELD joins *The Shooting Party* · JONATHAN KEATES returns to John Moore's Tewkesbury · SUE GEE visits the Poetry Bookshop · KEN HAIG takes the Tolkien Test